Quality Shareholders

Quality Shareholders
How the Best Managers Attract and Keep Them

Lawrence A. Cunningham

COLUMBIA UNIVERSITY PRESS

NEW YORK

Columbia University Press
Publishers Since 1893
New York   Chichester, West Sussex
cup.columbia.edu
Copyright © 2020 Lawrence A. Cunningham
All rights reserved

Library of Congress Cataloging-in-Publication Data

Names: Cunningham, Lawrence A., 1962– author.
Title: Quality shareholders : how the best managers attract
and keep them / Lawrence A. Cunningham.
Description: 1e. | New York City : Columbia University Press, 2020. |
Includes index.
Identifiers: LCCN 2020011456 (print) | LCCN 2020011457 (ebook) |
ISBN 9780231198806 (cloth) | ISBN 9780231552776 (ebook)
Subjects: LCSH: Stockholders. | Corporations—Investor relations. |
Investments. | Stocks.
Classification: LCC HD2744 .C86 2020 (print) | LCC HD2744 (ebook) |
DDC 659.2/85—dc23
LC record available at https://lccn.loc.gov/2020011456
LC ebook record available at https://lccn.loc.gov/2020011457

Columbia University Press books are printed on permanent
and durable acid-free paper.
Printed in the United States of America

Cover design: Noah Arlow
Cover image: Shutterstock

Quality is never an accident;
it is always the result of intelligent effort.
—John Ruskin

Contents

Contents

Contents

Quality Shareholders

The Shareholders Managers Deserve

IN 2013, SHAREHOLDER ACTIVIST TRIAN Partners and its leader, Nelson Peltz, targeted E. I. du Pont de Nemours & Co. (DuPont) and CEO Ellen Kullman. For two years, the sides debated DuPont's conglomerate structure, capital allocation, corporate overhead, and governance. When they hit a stalemate, Peltz nominated himself and three directors for the DuPont board at its annual shareholders' meeting on May 13, 2015. Peltz lost the battle by a thin margin; Kullman soon retired anyway, effectively losing the war; and DuPont morphed into Dow DuPont through a series of maneuvers. To this day, it is not obvious whether anyone "won," shareholders included.

The shareholder base was typical of today's U.S. public companies: besides insiders owning 0.3 percent and the activist having acquired 2.7 percent, DuPont was owned by a mix of index funds, short-term transients, long-term concentrated owners, pension funds, insurance companies, and individuals. Among larger holdings, ten of today's largest mutual funds commanded 33 percent of the vote. Both sides lobbied them intensively, spending $23 million between them.

The margin of "victory" was 3.5 percent,[1] meaning a different outcome if any one or two of those large shareholders switched sides. While it was natural for DuPont to swing into action when targeted, it could have vanquished its opponent had Kullman and her team cultivated a different shareholder base, one more in tune with her strategic vision for DuPont. Sculpting the shareholder base, bringing shareholders together, adds value in multiple ways for management, shareholders, and companies as a whole.

As an officer and director of a private corporation, I help decide whether or not to permit applicants to become fellow shareholders in our firm; as a public company director, neither I nor anyone else has such veto power. But while anyone can buy stock in a public company, that does not prevent companies from sculpting their shareholder base to attract some shareholders and repel others. In fact, given today's diversity of shareholder types based on time horizon and commitment levels, it is more important than ever to do so.

There are few ways public companies can prevent or expel given shareholders from buying or holding the stock. Through the 1980s, companies could buy out undesirable shareholders for a premium, a practice called "greenmail." Once used by incumbent boards targeted by corporate raiders, it's not been used for decades due to its odious character, unfavorable tax laws (gains are subject to punishing excise taxes), and more effective alternatives such as poison pills.

Short-termism remains a major concern. In the mid-1990s, a few rogue shareholders of Warren Buffett's Berkshire Hathaway planned to buy yet more of its pricey shares and deposit them into trusts that would, in turn, issue fractional interests at vastly lower unit prices. The trusts would attract short-term traders. That would undercut everything Buffett was trying to accomplish with Berkshire's cultivation of long-term committed shareholders.

To protect against that, Berkshire in 1996 effected a dual-class recap through which one class (the A class) would continue pretty much as before as a high-end stock, but a newly issued class (the B class) would bear fractional economic and voting interests and trade at a lower price. In this way, though Berkshire could not prevent the repellent shareholders from buying for themselves, it did inhibit them from buying at the levels needed for their unit trust plan. Short-term traders were deterred.

Indexers are today's dominant shareholder cohort—funds buy small stakes in all stocks in a defined index such as the S&P 500 or Russell 3000. While indexers helpfully offer the masses low-cost market returns, debate rages on whether they are capable of casting informed opinions in votes at the huge number of companies they hold stakes in. Managers sharing that concern can adopt policies that S&P and other index managers use to exclude companies from their index, such as dual-class voting, majority owners, or tracking stock.

Shareholder activists such as Peltz have since 2000 become a conspicuous, well-financed, and well-organized force in corporate life. Most officers and directors appreciate that the best way to avoid being targeted is to execute successfully on a reliable strategy delivering corporate prosperity. But it is equally important to ensure having a shareholder base that is more willing to agree with management, and its strategy, rather than one susceptible to an activist shareholder's challenges.

Many managers use their bully pulpit to deter shareholders unaligned with their corporate philosophy. At a Starbucks shareholders' meeting, Howard Schultz told a shareholder challenging the company's hiring practices that he should sell the stock. Joe Steinberg so advised a Leucadia shareholder challenging the company's hold-or-divest policies. In a 2014 letter to shareholders of the Washington Post Co., Don Graham stressed the company's long-term outlook, adding: "If you are a shareholder and YOU care about our quarterly results, perhaps you should think about selling the stock."

While hectoring can be an effective deterrence strategy, this book explores dozens of corporate practices and policies that shape the shareholder base to attract long-term committed owners. Examples: publishing long-term performance metrics; stating capital allocation policies; effecting strategic spin-offs; and establishing shareholder-oriented board selection criteria, voting arrangements, and executive pay practices. Managers can consciously deploy such tools to attract and reward desired shareholders and repel others.

While such shareholder cultivation is particularly valuable in today's world of fragmented shareholder demographics, it is a vintage art. It is well known to long-term committed shareholders and long practiced by the savvy managers who have succeeded in attracting them.

In his 1958 book, *Common Stocks and Uncommon Profits*, the legendary investor Phil Fisher likened companies to restaurants. Just as there are different kinds of restaurants, catering to different tastes, there are different kinds of companies, catering to different shareholder preferences.

In 1979, Buffett, renowned as both an investor and a chief executive, took Fisher's point a step further. Companies draw particular shareholders by communicating a specific corporate message. Backed by action, the message produces a self-selected shareholder base to match, along dimensions like time horizon, ownership levels, and engagement.

Today, every public company has a combination of different sorts of investors with varying appetites—long-term indexers, short-term transients, old-fashioned value investors, and—an omnipresent threat—activists.

Buffett has tried to attract only what he calls "high-quality" shareholders. These are defined as shareholders who buy large stakes and hold for long periods. They see themselves as part owners of a business, understand their businesses, and focus on long-term results, not short-term market prices. They contrast with indexers, who may hold for long periods but never concentrate, and transients, who sometimes hold large stakes but never for long—both of which invest comparatively little in understanding particular businesses.

Back in the 1980s, Berkshire attracted almost exclusively high-quality shareholders (hereafter shortened to QSs, which when plural can easily be pronounced as "cues"). Thanks to Buffett's menu—elaborated annually in his famous shareholder letters—98 percent of Berkshire shares outstanding at year-end were owned by those who owned at the beginning of the year. Over rolling five-year periods, at least 90 percent of Berkshire shareholders remained the same from year 1 to year 5. Almost all Berkshire shares were held by concentrated investors—their Berkshire holdings being twice their next largest stake in any other company.

Buffett's success in attracting QSs has been an important reason for Berkshire's success. They gave him a long-term runway, helped promote a rational stock price, and deterred shareholder activists from seeking to break up the conglomerate as it grew galactically. Berkshire dramatizes the tremendous results that can accrue when QSs match up with outstanding managers—and there are scores of such matchups in corporate America, as illustrated in this book. To repeat a popular paraphrase of Buffett's 1979 letter to Berkshire shareholders, "eventually, managers get the shareholders they deserve."

Berkshire's record of attracting QSs remains extraordinary. But today all those figures just referenced for Berkshire are lower, largely due to the changed and fragmented shareholder universe. Nowadays, index funds rule, though they were novelties through the 1990s. Up to 40 percent of public equity is now owned by declared indexers, or closet indexers, those proclaiming stock-picking prowess while maintaining sprawling portfolios that hug an index. Owning small stakes in hundreds or thousands of companies, indexers cannot understand the vast majority of their holdings.

Transient traders have long prowled stock markets, but average holding periods fell greatly through the early 2000s. They now average two to three years for most shareholder segments and less than one year for many. As a group, transients are as dominant as indexers, sporadically commanding up to 40 percent of total public equity too, and nearly as disadvantaged in understanding given companies. A rising portion of such transient trading is directed by artificial intelligence.[2]

This rise of indexers and transients created a vacuum in managerial accountability. Filling it are activist shareholders with a diverse range of horizons, commitments, and agendas. Variably controlling around 5 percent of total public equity, their campaigns amplify their influence.

Of course, all shareholders contribute to their corporate investees, starting with capital, and all stand to gain returns on capital. In fact, specific shareholder segments add unique value: activists promote management accountability, index funds enable millions to enjoy market returns at low cost, and traders offer liquidity.

With such assets, however, come liabilities: activists becoming overzealous, indexers lacking resources to understand specific company details, and traders inducing a short-term focus. A substantial cohort of QSs balances the shareholder mix and counteracts these liabilities.

As to curbing overzealous activism, QSs can be white squires. When a board perceives activist excess, it helps to have a few large long-term owners to consult. If they agree, the company's hand is strengthened, resisting excess while addressing legitimate concerns activist may have. In 2019, when Ashland Global Holdings received calls for a "strategic review" from an activist, it reached out to its QSs, including Neuberger Berman, who formed a united defensive front, and the activist withdrew.

QSs study company specifics that indexers, being stretched thin, cannot. Indexers may be good at analyzing dynamic issues as they arise, but they rarely develop the kind of deep knowledge that

QSs command. Indexers invest most of their limited resources to develop views about what is best generally in corporate governance, not what is best for particular companies.

Being long-term, QSs offset the short-term preferences of transients. Companies pressured to deliver results quickly benefit from QSs long-term horizons and patient capital. When Paul Polman of Unilever found in 2009 that the venerable company's shareholder list was dominated by transients, he began consciously cultivating QSs to change the base. By 2017, Unilever's base had a far greater density of QSs.

For officers and directors, having the right shareholders makes the difference not only between corporate prosperity and failure but personal success and setback. When a sizable QS cohort deters activists, incumbent management gains through less strife or distraction; when QSs vote based on company specifics rather than preconceived guidelines, incumbent managers are the beneficiaries; and QSs contribute to stock price rationality and a long runway for managers to execute strategy.

Finally, the long-term concentrated strategy of the QSs offers the potential for superior returns. True, the popular press often makes it seem as though passive index funds routinely beat managed funds after fees. And Buffett won a famous bet siding with indexers over hedge funds—at least those charging particularly high fees.[3] But the research is more nuanced and shows the merits of a skillful quality strategy that includes longer holding periods and higher concentration levels.

The rise of indexing, including its seemingly effortless strategy of investing along with its enormous power in voting, has crowded out the share of corporate equity held by QSs. The latter is down to as little as $4 trillion in assets, in all, compared to a total market capitalization exceeding $30 trillion.[4]

This book responds to the fact that the QS population has been shrinking. It stresses the untapped potential of QSs and offers methods to attract and cultivate them. The goals are to enlarge the cohort of QSs, to continue the education of current practitioners, and to add to the elite group of companies and leaders who attract them. While not strenuous, being a QS requires patience and diligence. While not arduous, attracting QSs is an ongoing project.

To explore QSs and the art of attracting them, this book draws on data and events to identify QSs, the companies that attract them most successfully, and why those companies are QS magnets. Such companies exist across all industries and the managers hail from diverse backgrounds—with slightly greater representation from the insurance industry and from managers who began their careers as investors. The upshot is that the practices presented here can be applied across the corporate landscape.

While this book's examples are drawn heavily from North America (Canada and the United States) and Europe (especially the United Kingdom), the insights and analysis will interest shareholders and managers throughout the world.[5] Shareholder fragmentation is a global phenomenon, along with the increasing power of indexers.[6] Related concerns will arise for all publicly traded companies, even in countries where significant equity stakes are held by the state (such as France), families (such as France and Italy), corporate agglomerations (such as Japan or Korea), or a more diverse constellation of global interests (such as China).

So complex is today's shareholder demographic that some say it is akin to the U.S. Electoral College—an arcane but powerful maze that intelligent candidates must master.[7] Just as presidential campaigns first lock up their base and then seek the swing voter, corporate leaders must first secure a faithful shareholder cohort and then assure any further votes that might determine voting outcomes. The map varies by company, but consists of QSs, indexers, transients, long-term concentrated owners, and activists. As in politics, these groups may be as reliable as California or Texas or as up for grabs as Ohio or Pennsylvania.

While the analogy is intriguing, there is one huge difference between political and corporate elections. Unlike politicians, who are stuck with the citizens they face, directors can influence the mix of the makeup of their shareholder base, in terms of such important features as time horizon, commitment level, and engagement.

Practices that attract QSs reflect a long-term business philosophy and owner orientation. They span the whole range of corporate affairs, from mission statements to governance philosophy, annual letters to succession planning, and capital allocation to executive compensation. The levers are available to every company, though adopting some entails mere tweaks in approach, while others require a shift in mindset. Each company must tailor these tools to suit its unique business and philosophy.

This book collates the practices and policies of scores of companies with demonstrated success in attracting QSs and illustrates for shareholders the cues and motifs of this art. No company follows every policy presented, and the practices are implemented differently in different hands and yield varying degrees of success.

Let's return to Phil Fisher's analogy between the corporate menu and the culinary one. Segment today's shareholders this way: quality (five-star) shareholders load up and stick around, transient (fast-food) shareholders stop in and speed away, and index (smorgasbord) funds may taste all but love none.

All have a place, but companies enjoy considerable flexibility writing their menus. In distilling the art of the QS, this book shows that QSs have a special place, which corporate leaders should appreciate as both discerning and desirable. Even with today's fragmented shareholder universe, managers can still get the shareholders they deserve. This book explains how, for managers and shareholders alike.[8]

PART I
Why Quality?

PART I INTRODUCES THE PROFILE of the QS and explains what distinguishes QSs from other investor types prevalent today. It follows with a catalogue of benefits that a high density of QSs offers. These include both comparative advantages in relation to other shareholder types and competitive advantages for the company's broader benefit. Comparative advantages are what QSs offer uniquely among shareholders, offsetting some downsides of fellow shareholder types—longer time horizons than transients, more informed voting than indexers, and more productive and patient engagement than activists. Competitive advantages from a high density of QSs include achieving high sustained returns on capital, rationality of stock pricing, and a brain trust to draw upon for board service and consultation.

1

Meet the Quality Shareholders

JOHN MAYNARD KEYNES, THE INTERNATIONAL economist and scholar, was the quintessential QS. Keynes stated his philosophy, based on years of experience and reflection: "I get more and more convinced that the right method in investments is to put fairly large sums" in select enterprises and that it is "a mistake to think that one limits one's risk by spreading too much between [diverse] enterprises."[1] Rather, Keynes explained, "I believe now that successful investment depends on . . . a steadfast holding of these in fairly large units through thick and thin, perhaps for several years."[2]

Keynes managed investments for Cambridge University's King's College from 1927 to 1945. He concentrated as much as half the portfolio in five companies and held them at least five years apiece.[3] Despite working in a challenging era that included the Great Depression and World War II, Keynes produced impressive returns: a compound annual growth rate of 9.12 percent in contrast to the broad U.K. market return of negative 0.89 percent.[4]

In the current era, a towering QS is Lou Simpson, who managed investments for Geico from 1979 to 2010. He was one reason Buffett opted to double Berkshire's investment in the car insurer in 1980 and buy the rest in 1995.[5] Simpson was both concentrated and patient, with a portfolio that averaged only eight to fifteen different companies, peaking at thirty-three in 1982, many held for decades.[6] Returns were stellar: Geico's average annual return on its equity portfolio during Simpson's tenure exceeded 20 percent versus a return on the S&P 500 of 13.5 percent.

Much has changed since Keynes's era and even since Simpson's heyday. But as another legendary investor, Benjamin Graham, often said, *plus ça change, plus c'est la même chose*—the more things change, the more they stay the same. Along with reviewing both the changing landscape and the constants, this chapter will highlight the distinctive features of the QS.

The Current Landscape

In decades past, shareholders seemed to be monolithic. In 1965, for example, institutional investors held $436 billion of $1.4 trillion in total market capitalization, with nearly $1 trillion owned by individual households. Managers could view individual stockholders as sharing similar interests, principally long-term corporate value, which gave managers broad discretion to pursue those interests. Less than 15 percent of the market, or $100 billion, was held by mutual funds, pension funds, and insurance companies (respectively holding $36, $43, and $21 billion—5 percent, 6 percent, and 3 percent).[7] The appetites of such firms did not differ greatly from one to the other or from those of individual investors.

Over the past several decades, shareholders have become increasingly diverse and far more demanding of managers. These range from indexers who buy everything to high-frequency traders who flip every minute. Some shareholder activists prescribe strategies for maximum short-term shareholder gain through divestitures, while socially oriented activists make shareholder proposals in the name of environmental, social, and governance objectives.

Several seismic forces contributed to the changed demographics. The broadest was the eclipse of individual shareholders by institutional investors. Since 2016, institutions have held the vast majority of the more than $30 trillion in total market capitalization, with mutual funds, pension funds, and insurance companies together commanding a decisive majority ($9.1 trillion, $2.3 trillion, and $811 billion, respectively).[8]

Among institutions, three critical changes have occurred in recent decades. Foremost, a large and growing percentage of shares are held by indexers. Indexing, popularized by the late Jack Bogle, was a marginal practice through the 1990s, but today is a familiar approach. His company, Vanguard, is a household name. Large indexers command trillions in assets, representing one-quarter to one-third or more of total U.S. public company equity. In 1997, less than 8 percent of mutual funds were indexed, whereas today more than 40 percent are.

Second is the substantial shortening of average holding periods, indicative of increased trading for arbitrage, momentum strategies, and other short-term drivers. Average holding periods shortened significantly from the mid-1960s through the early 2000s;[9] while the average has held steady since, this appears to be due to how the shorter horizons of many are offset by the more permanent holdings of the indexers.[10] Best-selling author Michael Lewis dramatized the stakes in his 2014 book *Flash Boys*, and the pace of acceleration continues with sustained technological advances in computing algorithms, artificial intelligence, and machine learning.[11]

Third is the rise of activism. Shareholder gadflies have roamed corporate America since the Gilbert brothers popularized the practice in the 1950s.[12] And from the 1970s through the 1990s, incumbent managers always faced constant threats to corporate control from rival firms, takeover artists, and colorful raiders such as Carl Icahn and Nelson Peltz.[13] But it is only in the past two decades that a vast pool of capital developed among specialty firms, dubbed shareholder activists, dedicated to the practice of featuring a well-developed playbook; a cadre of professional advisers; and repeat players such as Bill Ackman, Dan Loeb, and Paul Singer.[14]

With the rise and fragmentation of institutional investors, individual investors lost influence, while simultaneously diversifying themselves. Individual investors run the gamut from small retail holders to affluent sophisticates (called "high net worth"). Retail investors in turn may trade using TD Ameritrade or through brokers such as Merrill. The high net worth cohort varies widely too; some invest on their own, while others engage hedge funds, private equity firms, banks, or combinations of all three.

A further source of shareholder diversity for both individuals and institutions is tax sensitivity. Investors can be segmented by their exposure to capital gains taxes, based on measures of tax-motivated trading.[15] Tax-insensitive institutions command vastly more capital than tax-sensitive institutions. When tax rates are substantial, tax-sensitive institutions may have more interests in common with individuals—taxable people—than with other institutions.

The proliferation of institutional investors led to competition, with different investors adopting different styles. These included strategic focus—such as value, growth, or income—as well as ideal target size—such as small or large cap. Some funds combine these features and can be classified as large value, large growth, small value, or small growth. Yet another approach teases out trading styles and philosophy—such as momentum traders, technical traders, arbitrageurs, day traders, and high-speed traders.

Another feature of today's landscape is the diversity of shareholders, not all of which are focused on economic gain from their investments. For instance, the pension funds of the AFL-CIO advocate shareholder proposals that push a labor agenda.[16] The boards of public employee pension funds include government appointees and elected officials, all of whom respond to politics. Inverting the critical economic thought associated with Karl Marx, labor has never controlled so much capital.[17]

Despite this variety, the distinguishing feature of QSs has little to do with these alternatives. Instead, what distinguishes QSs from other shareholders is principally duration and concentration. They hold their investments far longer than average and concentrate their portfolios far more than average. Their chief contrasts are index investors, which might hold for long periods but never concentrate, and transients, which may occasionally load up, but rarely for long.

Such a classification system has a pedigree dating to the dawn of these dynamic changes in shareholder demographics. In 1998, Brian Bushee of the University of Pennsylvania Wharton School classified investors into similar cohorts: those prone to shorter time horizons and lower holding levels he dubbed *transients*, while those with longer holding periods and lower average stakes he labeled *indexers*.[18]

A third category to add to the matrix is *activist* shareholders. They tend to have higher average concentration—betting large on their targets—but shorter holding periods. Although some activist shareholders qualify as QSs as measured by concentration and commitment, most do not, and the cohort's more combative public engagement distinguishes its members from the QS pack.

Finally, the cohort Bushee calls *dedicated* corresponds to Buffett's *high-quality* shareholders and the *QSs* of this book.[19]

QSs Appeal

While each investor brings unique traits and habits to the exercise, a few hallmarks help define the QS.[20] The views of indexers, transients, and activists differ considerably from those of QSs.

Conviction. QSs view themselves as part owners of a business. Such an ownership sense requires conviction, reflected in thorough research and disciplined decisions. As the venerable firm of QSs, Ruane Cunniff put it: "We take pride and pleasure in investigating a company from all angles, doing the kind of on-the-ground, primary research that an enterprising journalist might do."[21]

QSs think about investments as businesses, not merely as securities, cash flows, or political instruments. Those who enjoy thinking about particular businesses (call this "microanalysis"), as opposed to stock markets as a whole or political economy generally ("macroanalysis"), benefit from this approach. There are vast differences between an emphasis on businesses and stocks and one on building stock portfolios or baskets of securities.

Patience. QSs are generally risk averse. Sustained patience reduces both reinvestment risk and expense risk. On reinvestment risk, selling shares results in capital needing to be reinvested, and finding new outstanding investments is time-consuming and difficult. On expense risk, trading and taxes are immediate costs of selling, disguising the stated nominal returns that draw attention. Owning outstanding companies for very long periods not only limits expense risk but reaps the benefits of compounding.

QSs are not motivated to beat the market in any given year but to generate returns over long periods of time. Steeled with patience and discipline, QSs sleep well at night. Untethered from slavish attendance to the index and unburdened by urgent trading needs, they favor low-volatility portfolios that can mostly tend themselves.

Engagement. A critical part of quality shareholding is a focused goal to develop and grow investee businesses through the supply of patient capital. This is an intangible benefit beloved by leaders of business innovation, from the assembly line and automobiles to artificial intelligence and autonomous vehicles.

QSs are interested in promoting the best long-term interests of the corporation and its shareholders. They are not proponents of parochial or political agendas on matters extraneous to the corporate mission or managerial skill set.

QSs Versus Indexers.[22] Indexers believe in efficient markets in which share prices reflect future prospects. QSs doubt that numbers capture all, whether computed by humans, powerful computers, or elaborate algorithms. Passive investing is great for delivering low-cost market returns, but is not favored by QSs.

Efficient markets—those with prices rationally related to business value—will be promoted by shareholders who study fundamental information to form the best judgments of value. By the same token, the more that trading is done formulaically—by the likes of indexers—the less reliable stock prices are likely to be.[23] QSs conduct the fundamental analysis that is necessary to promote stock market efficiency. Passive funds free ride on that work.

QSs Versus Transients. At the other extreme, transients (active or hyperactive fund managers) play at outfoxing one another, rather than carefully deploying capital. Transient shareholders help to set market price, but when this result is due more to frenetic action than dispassionate analysis, that price is more apt to be higher or lower than intrinsic value. The distracting competition appears to be one reason why so many cannot beat the market returns of mere indexers, at least not after subtracting fees. This failure helps explain why so many investors have migrated to indexing—many doing so secretly in the practice criticized as "closet indexing."

QSs reject this capitulation, insisting on practicing more traditional investing. They aspire to secure the greatest long-term value for themselves and clients alike. Benefits are the returns, of course, as well as the growth of great companies. As another QS powerhouse, Baillie Gifford, puts it: "Investing responsibly for the long term is not counter to outperforming for clients, it's intrinsic to it."[24]

QSs Versus Activists. QSs are happy to engage with management, usually preferring to do so without making matters public. They leave that to the activists, although they are prepared to support activists as appropriate and to speak publicly when necessary.[25] After all, each activism campaign presents a unique set of conditions that have combined to create an inflection point for a target.

Activists deserve a hearing that management should be willing to entertain, so long as they can make a case for value creation based on the merits. In all events, QSs make independent decisions on shareholder votes, not retaining outside partners or deferring to proxy adviser recommendations (although reading the latter's research can help them become fully informed of the variety of relevant views).

Engagement styles aside, activists can also be quality. Three noted shareholder activists, for instance, rank high in combined commitment and concentration: Pershing Square, Third Point, and ValueAct.[26]

That said, managers and directors are far more interested in attracting non-activist QSs than activists. Indeed, one reason to cultivate QSs is to deter activism; one point of this book is to show how all shareholders might embrace QS traits more widely.

The Shareholder Universe

Today's institutional investors face enormous pressure to favor indexing or transience. Compensation of fund managers is often based on annual returns, so the question always becomes whether an investor beat the market for a given year or not. In such an environment, pressure is substantial to diversify widely on the one hand and to chase returns by rapid trading on the other. The result is a rising portion of indexers and transients compared to QSs.

The effects of this intensive environment are reflected in estimates of the relative size of these cohorts. The number of different indexes has proliferated—at least sixty major ones by one count, with Morningstar alone designating at least three hundred different indexes.[27] Self-described index funds easily manage at

Table 1.1
Today's shareholder cohorts

		INVESTMENT CONCENTRATION	
		Lower	Higher
INVESTMENT HORIZON	Shorter	Transients (40%)	Activists (5%)
	Longer	Indexers (40%)	Quality (15%)

least 20 percent of total market capitalization, a figure that rises to as much as 40 percent if funds that hug indexes without describing themselves as index funds are counted (Table 1.1).

Transient holders are numerous, reflected in high share turnover. In the past two decades, average holding periods for hedge funds have fallen to under one year, and for mutual funds under two.[28] Together, this transient cohort represents perhaps as much as 40 percent of total market capitalization as well.[29]

At the other extreme, activists command relatively small stakes, likely not more than 5 percent of all, though they strategically leverage their power during campaigns. QSs make up the rest. While small overall—perhaps 15 percent of all equity—this cohort can be mobilized for amplified influence.

The QS Edge

Substantial research is devoted to assessing the relative success of different shareholder approaches. Investors and researchers have long debated, for example, the relative success of investors adopting a "value" strategy versus a "growth" strategy.[30]

For nearly two decades, debate has raged around whether stock indexing or stock picking is a superior strategy. The broad debate is often extended further into specific types of indexes (by size, sector, or geography) with stock pickers competing against that benchmark.[31]

Debate dates to a 1997 article by Mark Carhart that found no evidence of successful mutual fund stock pickers.[32] Ensuing research contributed to what became conventional wisdom: average active funds underperform the market after fees;[33] top fund performance doesn't persist;[34] and, while some managers are skilled, few deliver on that value for customers after fees.[35]

But changes in shareholder demographics during the past two decades, including increased competition and lower fees, has produced a new strand of research challenging these conventional views. For instance, there is evidence that the average active fund does outperform an equivalent index;[36] some top-performance records do persist;[37] and a sizable cohort of managers with particular traits demonstrate skill that justifies their fees.[38] Among those traits are conviction and patience, the defining traits of QSs. Based on this evidence, it is quite possible for skillful QSs to systematically outperform too.[39] The QS firm Lyrical Asset Management has reported superior results simply from a strategy of five-year minimum holding periods of stocks outside the largest ones scooped into all the indices.

Beyond the academic literature, popular writers on the debate concur. Consider Larry Swedroe, author of *Disappearing Alpha*, explaining the increasing difficulty of successful stock picking. While still preferring stock indexing to stock picking, Swedroe concedes that there is a "compelling case" that stock pickers do best when they are patient and selective—the essential attributes of QSs.[40] Likewise, the distinguished editor of the *Alpha Architect* blog, Wesley Gray, an unabashed devotee of the conventional academic literature favoring indexing, stresses equally the evidence supporting committed long-term investors such as QSs.[41]

In the popular trade book arena, debate has continued for several decades. Multiple editions of best-selling books continue to showcase dueling university professors. For instance, University of Pennsylvania professor Jeremy Siegel has repeatedly shown that buy and hold works,[42] while Princeton University professor

Burton Malkiel continues to release new editions of the book that legitimized indexing as a strategy.[43]

Another best-selling author, Howard Marks, a champion QS himself, has stressed the perils of too much indexing for markets. Because indexes never appraise value and buy simply based on inclusion/exclusion and relative size of companies across an index, they breed price distortion. Only non-indexers contribute to the valuation assessments everyone relies on markets to produce. Marks stresses a silver lining: more indexing creates more opportunities for QSs.[44]

Some QSs make a point of hunting for companies that are not included in major indices. All indexes use a variety of screens to determine which companies to include and which to exclude. Principal examples are size by market capitalization (hence the S&P "500" or Russell "3000"). But there are less obvious screens that exclude, ranging from geography to capital structure.

A prominent hunter is the Boyar Value Group, a fixture for decades in the QS community, whose research report subscribers comprise a substantial segment of the QS cohort. Referring to this group of companies as "index orphans," Boyar has identified some 750 public companies of this sort—all with market capitalizations exceeding $1 billion and sixty exceeding $10 billion—examples being IAC/InterActiveCorp, Axalta Coating Systems, Madison Square Garden Company, and MSG Networks.[45]

While debate continues, many thousands of stock pickers vie for advantage in the hunt for outstanding businesses. This book is intended to help them in their search while also helping managers and directors learn how to attract them.[46]

Both companies and markets benefit from a mix of shareholder types. In fact, the adverse effects of some shareholder cohorts may be offset by the contributions of others. That's certainly true in the case of QSs, as the next chapter explains.

2

Comparative Advantages

Dear Fellow TICC Stockholders,

TIME IS RUNNING OUT. You must act now to seize on the opportunity to finally end the failed performance of the external adviser of TICC Capital Corp. ("TICC").

Listen to the outside proxy advisors. Do not listen to management's self-interested arguments. All three leading proxy advisory firms have called for TICC stockholders to support TSLX's campaign for change at TICC.

In this campaign by TSLX (also known as TPG Specialty Lending) to make changes at TICC Capital, the challenger made a strong push for shareholder support:

*Stockholders, **YOU** have the power to effect change at TICC and protect your investment. **YOU** are the true owners of the Company and **YOU** should exercise your right to **VOTE** the **GOLD** card in favor of TSLX's proposals.*

Management pushed back equally hard. The shareholders split nearly evenly. By a voting margin of less than 1 percent, TICC lost the battle. This case shows how important the shareholder base is, how it can determine the outcome of a fight between activists and incumbents.

Even Procter & Gamble, with a market capitalization exceeding $200 billion, fought a pitched proxy battle to an indefinite conclusion involving recounts of the voting separated by a paper-thin margin: 44,000 shares of 2 billion that were voted, a mere 0.0016 percent.

While all shareholders offer the benefit of capital, liquidity, and a valuation, in today's landscape, shareholder type matters. Shareholders have a lot more power than they used to and they wield it from every angle. And such power has been professionalized and institutionalized in the form of shareholder activism, short-termism, and proxy advisers—all which offer benefits but come with liabilities.

QSs can offset the side effects of short-term transients, over-zealous activists, and indexers who rely on proxy advisers. At the same time, QSs will not merely follow management but engage in active discussions and make informed decisions.

Offsetting Transient Time Pressures

Managers need leeway as well as capital. Significant corporate projects require time to develop, implement, and evaluate. That's true of new products as well as bolt-on acquisitions. Proof of corporate strategy usually manifests over years not quarters, whether focused on enhancing the consumer experience or rolling up an industry.

Shareholders who supply capital and then give way enable managers to perfect projects and execute on strategy. Those endlessly trading or second-guessing do not. Accountability must be maintained, but there is a balance that QSs respect.

A good example is the shareholders of Amazon.com, consciously cultivated by founder Jeff Bezos. In 1997, he took Amazon public as an online bookseller. The company conquered that market and, over the next decades, reinvested every dollar in a diverse array of powerful innovations, from e-books to cloud computing.

For many years, the company struggled to achieve positive earnings and, even when it generated profits, margins were thin. Yet shareholders cheered. Even amid earnings declines from period to period, when accompanied by reported R&D investment and long-term growth plans, Amazon's stock price rose to reflect the market's faith in its long-term value.

Bezos made the long-term vision clear from the outset and never wavered—nor has a core of QSs in Amazon's shareholder base. As Bezos wrote in his 1997 letter to Amazon's new shareholders, which he has attached to every annual letter since: "It's All About the Long Term." Bezos had the advantage of starting with a clean slate, but older companies can make a course correction to focus on the long term.

In 2009, hoary old Unilever's share turnover mapped that of other multinationals, plagued by a large portion of shareholders with holding periods of less than one year.[1] To CEO Paul Polman, the high level of transients translated into urgent demands for maximizing quarterly profits and daily share prices.

Such a capital market outlook adversely affected operations, strategy, and reporting. Unilever published quarterly earnings guidance, forming expectations among market watchers. Then, to meet these expectations, division managers cut spending on R&D, information technology, and capital projects.

Polman recognized this flawed strategy. He adopted new policies and clearly communicated these to shareholders and the market. Unilever would cease quarterly guidance and reporting. It would no longer seek to deliver maximum profits each quarter or year but would seek consistent and sustained profits across multiple years. At first, the stock price dropped.

But within two years, it recovered and continued to rise over the next eight years, in tandem with sustained profits. In the process, transient shareholders were chased away, replaced by a concentration of long-term shareholders. As of late 2017, not long before Polman retired, Unilever's fifty largest owners boasted an average holding period of seven years.[2]

Transient pressure is real. It can lead boards to extraordinary measures. For a dramatic illustration, consider the 2011 battle waged by Air Products for control of Airgas. As bidding rose to $70 per share, many Airgas shareholders, including some QSs, sold. With almost half the remaining shares in the hands of transients, the Airgas board expressed concern that they would simply accept the $70 bid despite the company's greater long-term value.

When Airgas's board tried to thwart the Air Products bid, a court battle ensued. Despite some skepticism—noting that many long-term holders had sold to the transients—the judge agreed with the board. After all, the judge noted, Air Products' own experts had acknowledged that many transients would sell at $70, even if they thought Airgas's long-term value was greater.

In short, while transients may cast their lot according to immediate cash values, QSs take the long view. They always consider and generally support valid management plans over multiple time periods, giving due consideration to building value. If boards, such as Airgas's, can consider transient dominance to defeat hostile tender offers, they certainly can evaluate how their ordinary business judgments shape the shareholder base.

Countering Indexer Influence

Most shareholder meeting votes are routine and pass with wide margins. But at least a few hundred annually are close calls. One study of shareholder voting from 1997 to 2004 found that more than seven hundred were decided by a margin of less than 10 percent.[3]

Another study covering shareholder proposals on corporate governance from 2003 to 2016 reported evidence that managers exert considerable effort toward proposals decided by narrow margins, winning three times as many as they lose.[4] Such results underscore the value to managers of planning for such occasions.

Public companies disclose substantial information, which analysts dissect, and then use to generate more. QSs regularly produce, gather, and analyze this information. They continually update it to be prepared to cast informed votes on any corporate matter that may arise.

Indexers, in contrast, lack such ongoing examination processes. Instead, when an especially significant vote is scheduled, they convene cram sessions. They compare information assembled by others with their preexisting guidelines and cast votes accordingly. On more routine votes, indexers tend to vote based on standards stated in their preexisting guidelines.

The business model of the large index funds is to develop a broad portfolio of securities, minimize costs, and match the index. Compensation is based on the size of the fund rather than the performance of the fund. Accordingly, indexers strive to increase assets under management (AUM).

The result is a focus on the aggregate market, rather than the needs of particular companies. Indexers can be expected to engage as shareholders only to the extent that the benefits from doing so extend across the entire portfolio—the whole index. Among the large cohort of index investors, almost all adopt general guidelines that determine how they cast their votes.

Governance intervention must be based on an assumption that the item is good for the whole portfolio, presumably in terms of economic performance. Performance intervention must be based on an assumption that supporting a challenge to a particular company will affect managerial behavior across the portfolio.

Large indexers have their champions, of course. Some argue that their size provides vast economies of scale and scope to grasp issues quickly across many diverse companies.[5] Others contend that their incentive to increase AUM alone suffices to assure casting informed votes—the greater a company's market capitalization, the more AUM indexers own in it, and the higher their fees, this argument goes.[6] The industry and its fans emphasize substantial behind-the-scenes avenues of engagement outside the limelight.[7] They point to how the largest three have publicized their decisions to increase their stewardship staff, even doubling the head count in one case.

Critics question these assertions. Concerning maximizing AUM, of course, it is not in the interests of shareholders simply to grow—retaining and deploying earnings in suboptimal projects does that while hurting shareholders. At many companies, shareholders are best served not by increasing size but by dividends, buybacks, divestitures, spin-offs, and other techniques that reduce rather than increase corporate size.

For instance, the Washington Post Co. in 2015 spun off its Cable One subsidiary, renaming the remaining company Graham Holdings.[8] Cable One began trading at around $400 per share and today is worth $1,500. Indexers focused on Graham as a factor in AUM might have balked at this extraordinarily valuable transaction. We will discuss the topic of capital allocation in part II—a vital topic dear to QSs, yet so often myopically ignored by indexers and their supporters alike.

As troubling for supporters is the small staff size—even after the vaunted increases—in relation to the number and size of companies to be followed. Among the largest indexers, BlackRock doubled its stewardship staff to forty-five; Vanguard has twenty-one; and State Street has twelve. Yet these indexers have holdings in more than eleven thousand companies each worldwide, and at least three thousand in the U.S. alone. They cast votes at more than four thousand annual meetings adding up to more than thirty thousand proposals.

Put in dollar terms, total stewardship investment is about $13.5 million, $6.3 million, and $3.6 million, respectively, all less

Table 2.1
Indexers' limited stewardship stakes

	BlackRock	Vanguard	State Street
Stewardship staff	45	21	12
Investees worldwide	11,246	13,225	12,191
Investees U.S.	3,765	3,672	3,117
Maximum person-days	<4	<2	<2
Stewardship expense	$13.5 million	$6.3 million	$3.6 million
Total fees and expenses	$9.1 billion	$3.5 billion	$2.6 billion

Note: See Lucian Bebchuk and Scott Hirst, "Index Funds and the Future of Corporate Governance: Theory, Evidence, and Policy," *Columbia Law Review* 119 (2019): 2029–146 (compiling data from Morningstar).

than one-fifth of 1 percent—only 0.2 percent—of total fees and expenses. Even if the staff focused only on the largest companies—say, where their stakes exceed $1 billion, which still adds to hundreds—they could only devote two to four person-days per year studying them.

Table 2.1 presents a stark picture.

For context, consider the head count at two other companies involved in investment analysis. Moody's, the bond-rating agency covering a large swath of capital markets, employs 12,000 people. Among the largest QSs, Capital Research keeps up with a far smaller portfolio of companies, 7,500.

Even assuming vast economies of scale or scope and motivation to boost AUM, it is hard for many to believe that such limited resources suffice to yield informed opinions on the tens of thousands of shareholder decisions required of an owner of shares in many thousands of companies. While many decisions are quotidian, at least a significant portion would require some knowledge that would entail reading the annual report and proxy statement and determining the company's strategic plan and past performance, components of its executive compensation plans, and pending shareholder and management proposals. Yet the evidence indicates that even the big indexers access only 29 percent of governance-related public filings of their investees.[9]

When it comes to so-called private engagement, the probabilities and public record point to inherent limitations. From 2017 through 2019, the largest indexers reported having multiple annual engagements with only a handful of their investees— 3.9 percent at BlackRock, 2.3 percent at Vanguard, and 0.6 percent at State Street; they had just one engagement with another 7.2 percent, 3.5 percent, and 5.0 percent, respectively.[10] In other words, over a recent three-year period, these firms had no engagement with the overwhelming majority of the companies they invest in.

Despite all this, the large indexers exert inordinate influence. Three referenced indexers own sizable stakes in virtually every large public company, routinely controlling 20 percent or more of the vote. Therefore, it is especially vital for such companies to attract a substantial cohort of QSs to offset the resulting power wielded by indexers, whose focus is on the entire market rather than a particular company.

Consider Capital One, whose largest shareholders include the following QSs (with rough percentage of portfolio and percent of the company in parentheses): Dodge & Cox (3, 9), Capital World Investors (1, 8), Davis Selected Advisers (6, 3), Franklin Resources (.6, 3), Harris Associates (Oakmark Funds) (1.4, 1.8), and Hotchkis & Wiley (1.6, 1). Altogether, these QSs command nearly one-fourth of the vote, a stronger force in Capital One than its largest indexers together command—a rare feat in corporate America today.

On the other hand, even many wonderful companies face opposite demographics today. Consider Genuine Parts, a century-old distributor of automotive parts with an impressive long-term record of performance and attracting QSs. Three dozen of its shareholders stake more than 1 percent of their portfolios in the stock, many for decades. The cohort's holdings together aggregate 11 percent of the vote, an impressive block that can be expected to vote in an informed manner in the company's best long-term economic interests. But the company's three largest indexers together command 27 percent, and three other large indexers together hold 10 percent more. These shareholder demographics underscore how the fate of even impressive companies with large clusters of QSs may often be decided by indexers.

Many index funds are influenced by the centralized voting recommendations of the two large proxy advisory firms, Institutional Shareholder Services (ISS) and Glass Lewis, which control 97 percent of the proxy advisory market. As with the large index firms, the advisers' voting recommendations reflect what is seen as best for a portfolio of securities rather than a particular company. For example, guidelines generally promote certain precepts for all companies: splitting the roles of board chairman and CEO, cumulative voting, and shareholder action by written consent.

The guideline approach is necessary, because these advisers are stretched thin—though perhaps not as badly as the largest indexers. They operate with lean staffs on low budgets, and just 1,000 employees at ISS and 1,200 at Glass Lewis. Yet they address a huge market: ISS boasts 1,700 institutional clients while Glass Lewis's clients together manage $35 trillion in assets. Their small crews opine on hundreds of thousands of separate decisions annually—ISS addresses 40,000 annual meetings and Glass Lewis 20,000.

Measuring the exact influence of ISS and Glass Lewis is difficult, because some investors might vote the same way anyhow. But estimates range from swaying 6 percent to 33 percent of any given vote—significant when one considers that many are decided by small margins. Evidence also shows that institutional investors are substantially more inclined to vote for proposals that advisers support than oppose—by margins ranging from 16 to 27 percent on executive compensation to 64 to 73 percent on directors in contested elections.[11]

Research indicates that while proxy adviser recommendations tailored to particular cases often add value for shareholders, those based on general guidance without specific research do not.[12] In such cases, it falls to QSs to counter the effects of ill-advised proxy adviser recommendations.

An inference of influence appears in the widely followed 2019 annual meeting of UBS, where management narrowly lost a vote on what is usually an easily approved formality. The vote was over a proposal to discharge directors from personal liability for money damages the company might pay in court—a routine matter for American and European companies alike. It became an issue for UBS after a French court found the company liable for abetting tax evasion by high net worth clients.

UBS shareholders, which include a large cohort of U.S. investors, many holding large blocks for long terms, approved most matters with more than 90 percent of the vote—auditor appointment, financial statements, and dividend and board elections. But they rejected the discharge proposal with nearly an equal percentage for as against (42 percent), with about 16 percent abstaining (a majority being needed for the vote to carry). The shareholders also sent a protest vote concerning say on pay, with just more than 81 percent voting *yes*.

These outcomes suggest that many shareholders responded to recommendations of the proxy advisory firms. On discharge, ISS had advised voting against, while Glass Lewis advised abstaining; Glass Lewis also advised voting against on pay.[13] Thus a roughly similar portion of votes concurred with Glass Lewis— nearly 17 percent on discharge and about 19 percent on pay. If so, the discharge vote might well have been different had Glass

Lewis supported it. Similarly, management would more likely have prevailed had it enjoyed a deeper bench of QSs compared to indexers who subscribe to the proxy advisers.

The all-time loser for blind adherence to proxy adviser general guidelines remains the 2005 recommendation of ISS to withhold votes for Warren Buffett as a director of Coca-Cola. Buffett's Berkshire Hathaway bought a large stake in the company in 1988, representing in 2005 a large portion of both Coca-Cola's outstanding stock and Berkshire's securities portfolio. Despite that clear alignment with the interests of fellow shareholders, ISS refused to support Buffett as a director by asserting a conflict of interest between Coca-Cola and various Berkshire subsidiaries, including Dairy Queen, a customer.

Buffett objected, stressing how Berkshire's large and lengthy stock ownership dwarfed the routine business transactions of its subsidiaries. In the ensuing board election, 16 percent of Coca-Cola's shares were cast as withhold votes on Buffett, so he was reelected, but he nevertheless opted to stand down.

More recently, consider an ISS rule that caps the number of public boards a director may serve on—five for most directors, three for those who are also public company CEOs serving on their own boards. In 2019, the rule prompted a withhold recommendation on Tom Gayner, CEO and director of Markel Corporation. Gayner has been on the boards of two businesses once part of the Washington Post Co. and Colfax Corporation, a Danaher spin-off—a total of four—so ISS withheld support.

ISS's withhold recommendation was formulaic not substantive; it was about the number of boards not the person and ignored how the number arose solely from reconfiguration of the Washington Post Co. Half the votes were withheld, despite Gayner being among America's most distinguished businessmen, known for a philosophy and record akin to that of Buffett.[14] In contrast, Gayner was handily reappointed to his own board of Markel, which boasts a high density of QSs.

In short, corporations should not rely heavily on the indexers to cast informed shareholder votes but should look more to QSs to promote optimal voting.

Curbing Overzealous Activism

In the heyday of hostile corporate takeovers, incumbents leaned on shareholders for support, securing friendly blocks of white squires. Participants included Ken Miller's Lodestar Group, Harris Associates, Roy Disney's Trefoil Capital Investors, and Lazard Frères' Corporate Partners.[15] Today, however, attracting QSs is among the best defenses against overzealous shareholder activism.

Close calls arise in many activist proxy contests. In 2006, for instance, Nelson Peltz was elected to the H. J. Heinz Company board by a small margin. In 2008, vote counts in two major contests were so close they had to be conducted twice—the 3G campaign against CSX[16] and Carl Icahn's intervention against Yahoo.

With stakes like those—also featured in the battles noted earlier involving DuPont, Procter & Gamble, and TICC Capital—the vote of every shareholder counts.[17] Knowing this, activists consider shareholder voting propensities when evaluating targets. By the same token, it pays for incumbents to cultivate a shareholder base of likely supporters. The quality of the shareholder list can be the difference between victory and defeat.

In choosing targets, activists focus primarily on business quality, pricing, and catalysts to increase value. They often own as little as 1 or 2 percent and rarely more than 5 percent. Activists therefore review ownership structure of potential targets and are deterred by companies boasting substantial shareholders likely to oppose proposed strategies.[18] A large cohort of QSs can be a strong deterrent.

In 2018, activists at Elliott Management signaled impatience with managers of Pernod Ricard, the spirits firm with a substantial

(16 percent) family ownership. One of its QSs is Tom Russo, who manages $12 billion at Gardner, Russo & Gardner, including $850 million worth of Pernod Ricard shares. He weighed in publicly:[19]

> "You have a classic case of a business that could show a lot more today, if they chose to," said Tom Russo. "I still think our best course of action is to invest meaningfully at the expense of operating margin today for more wealth tomorrow."

In 2019, Ashland Global Holdings called upon some of its higher QSs to respond to an unwanted activist overture. Cruiser Capital, a hedge fund that had acquired 2.5 percent of the shares, nominated four directors to the chemical company's board, seeking to oust four incumbents. In response, the company reached out to its major QSs, including Neuberger Berman, a shareholder of at least five years with 2.8 percent of the shares.

As a result of those consultations with QSs, the company proposed an alternative reconfiguration of the board, putting the activist off balance. The activist soon withdrew its proposals. The company agreed it could participate with the other shareholders in identifying two new outside directors. The company also hired an industry consultant.

Shareholders who understand and appreciate a company's business model are attractive, especially for those companies following a structure or strategy that bucks prevailing fashions. For example, activist investors often urge razor-sharp focus, criticize diverse operations, and oppose conglomerates. While outcomes vary, having a substantial contingent of QSs helps managers navigate the pressure, creating both time and options.

Consider 3M, a sprawling conglomerate boasting sixty thousand products backed by ninety-three thousand employees across multiple sectors, including consumer, health care, transportation, electronics, and safety. While other conglomerates have broken up, it has expanded. This contrarian strategy may be related to a distinctive engineering culture focused on research, development, and innovation.[20] It is certainly helped by a high density of QSs; its largest shareholders, besides the big indexers, are QS stalwarts, with a half dozen together owning nearly 8 percent of the stock.[21]

Another conglomerate benefiting from its large QS cohort is Illinois Tool Works (ITW). It is a diverse industrial agglomeration of nearly eight hundred different businesses assembled over decades through acquisition, and it operates in a decentralized manner. In 2012, pointing to the argument for industry focus and a share price lagging business value, the activist firm Relational Investors questioned the model. While the two sides clashed publicly, they ultimately compromised, strongly on ITW's terms. Relational won a single board seat, while ITW divested thirty businesses and consolidated the rest into ninety units over the next four years. Despite the changes, its century-old business model remained intact.

ITW could not have managed this feat without shareholders who respected the business model and embraced it, and a CEO, Scott Santi, able both to explain the model and activate it. That shareholder base, leading with a 6 percent holding in the trust of the founding family (Briar Hall Management), boasts not only the typical mix of passive and actively managed financial behemoths, but many QSs with meaningful ownership of the company, such as State Farm Insurance, which owned a stake exceeding 5 percent for many years.

The drumbeat against conglomerates remains alive, with United Technologies (UTX) targeted in a campaign begun in early 2018. Management took a patient approach to evaluating options, studying alternatives for nearly a year before developing an elaborate program of both divestiture and acquisition on management's terms and timetable.[22]

Helping hold the activists at bay were a QS base that dwarfed the activists' holdings: whereas the activists, staking large portions of their capital, held only 1.62 percent of UTX stock, as few as eight QSs together owned 7 percent.[23] While the activists continued to criticize the transactions, especially the ultimate step of UTX merging with Raytheon, UTX management reached out to its QSs and got their support.[24] The managers appealed to the QSs's time horizon, arguing that any shareholder with at least a five-year investment horizon should support the transactions.[25]

No Rubber Stamps

QSs will not, of course, rubber-stamp any management proposal, nor should they. That is especially so when management is on one side and shareholders on the other. Consider Dell Inc.'s 2013 going private transaction. Founder Michael Dell offered a price that many shareholders considered too low. A fierce valuation battle ensued, pitting Dell against such venerable QSs as T. Rowe Price and Southeastern Asset Management (as well as activist Carl Icahn). Dell narrowly eked out the required shareholder vote.

Nor can QSs be counted on to work in lockstep with one another—a reason to cultivate a large number of them. Consider, for instance, the case of RenaissanceRe (RenRe), a reinsurer based in Bermuda and listed on the New York Stock Exchange. Among its QSs is TimesSquare Capital, a shareholder since at least 2010, holding 2.4 percent and often productively engaged. But in 2018, it publicly prescribed a strategic review, a move that activists commonly make. In response, RenRe made two moves to increase the holdings of two other QSs to a combined 9 percent as white squires: it issued a large new equity stake to long-term business partner and venerable QS State Farm Insurance and closed a pending acquisition of Tokio Marine, paying partly in stock. TimesSquare quietly retreated.

Yet QSs may be more likely than professional activists to cooperate amid disagreement. M&G, a U.K. pension fund in business for nearly a century, is a quintessential QS. For more than a decade, it was the largest shareholder of Methanex Corporation, owning in 2019 a 16 percent stake in the Canadian methane producer. That's when management unveiled a huge capital project to build a massive new production facility in Louisiana, going it alone with substantial leverage. M&G, conservative by nature, voiced concerns of perennial risk of price declines in the commodity business that could not only jeopardize completing the huge project but threaten insolvency.

In response, the Methanex board chairman told M&G if they did not like the strategy, they should sell their shares. While such a "Wall Street rule" reigned in decades past, this option is no longer viable in many cases. In the case of Methanex, not a widely held stock, it would have taken several years for M&G to sell all its shares. So M&G went activist, nominating a short slate of four independent directors for the upcoming annual meeting. (I was one of the nominees.) After a brief period of public skirmishing over the disagreement, Methanex and M&G settled on terms appointing one nominee to the board and agreeing to name another shortly. After obtaining additional review and assurance, the company proceeded with the plant.

These examples illustrate the importance of a shareholder who understands the company from all sides. The QS is that shareholder who will act in the best interests of the company—whether that means challenging management or cooperating with it.

Attracting a substantial cohort of QSs offers the benefit of counteracting the downside of other shareholder groups who gain from the "megaphone effect." It can also be a competitive advantage that radiates to many different aspects of the company, as chapter 3 explains.

3

Competitive Advantages

AMONG PIONEERS OF THE STRATEGY of sustainable competitive advantages was business professor Michael Porter. His 1980 book, *Competitive Strategy*, remains canonical. Porter described the five forces companies must defend against: zeal of competitors; bargaining power of suppliers and customers; and ease of substitutes for the company's offerings and entry of voracious rivals.[1]

As these forces remain constant threats, Porter explained that companies must create competitive advantages—often called "moats"—to fortify themselves. QSs contribute many such advantages, as the by-product of their patient engaged approach, spanning from philosophy and relationships to rationality, strategy, and even succession.

Philosophy

Porter identified industry structure as a factor to be considered when sizing up competitive advantage. Companies in dynamic fragmented industries—such as ride-sharing or workspace leasing—often have many hungry aspirants inclined to cutthroat behavior. Resulting price wars can erode profit margins. While all industries see bursts of irrationality, companies in industries with rational competitors, such as stodgy oligopolistic ones, enjoy a moat that discourages impoverishing market share battles. Economic returns ebb or flow accordingly.

For managers to withstand such shortsighted irrationality, it helps to have an understanding shareholder base, one that will be patient through the pressure. Across industry structures, the presence of QSs can help resist both the pervasive battles and the occasional outbursts of irrationality. Amazon and its shareholders are a case in point: the company and its QSs endured many business challenges together over more than a decade, but the shareholder base stuck with them, and eventually it paid off. A critical mass of QSs builds a moat; adding to the QS rolls deepens that moat.

Attracting a high density of QSs with their characteristic patience can be a direct benefit to a company. The presence of QSs is associated with managers using strategic rather than merely tactical competitive actions.[2] Many CEOs who have attracted a high density of QSs cite the QS role as essential to being able to maintain a long-term outlook.

One example is Markel Corporation, a third generation Richmond-based insurance company. Consider this point made in Markel's 2016 letter to shareholders: "We believe that Markel remains unique among most publicly traded companies in emphasizing the forever time horizon as much as we do. That is an immense competitive advantage [that] very few organizations enjoy. . . . The only reason we remain free to do so is that you, our shareholders, have placed an immense amount of trust in us."

Others have stressed the similar point about how providing patient capital can be a moat. Leucadia National, a diversified holding company begun in 1979 by Ian Cumming and Joe Steinberg, reflected in a 2014 letter to shareholders: "One of our biggest competitive advantages is our permanent capital base, complemented by our focus on the long-term, which is ingrained in the management teams."

In addition, the patience of QSs percolates throughout a company. If less pressure comes from shareholders to produce short-term results, then directors, officers, employees, suppliers, strategic partners, and others can operate in the same manner. They can take the time they need to execute their mission, from strategy to production and sales.[3]

Markel, led by Tom Gayner, is both a QS of its large investment portfolio and an attractor of a high-density QS base. The company consciously cultivates this cohort, which it calls the "right owners." Markel considers them a competitive advantage:

Having the right owners with a suitable long term time horizon provides us with an immense competitive advantage. In today's world, short term and artificial time pressures permeate too many decisions. Our dual time horizon of Forever and Right Now allows us to make necessary Right Now decisions on a day by day basis. But we always get to make those decisions with the Forever mindset guiding us while we do so. That is an incredibly rare advantage in today's world. It would not happen without you as long term committed owners. For that we are greatly appreciative. Thank you.[4]

Relationships

Companies gain considerable competitive advantages by building strong commercial relationships. These are conventionally thought of in terms of manufacturers, distributors, suppliers, customers, and lenders.

Because QSs know their investee companies so well and are substantially invested in their success, they can be an additional

valuable relationship. A key way that QSs add value is by introducing directors for the board and serving as unpaid advisers.

For a classic example, look at the board of Teledyne, the conglomerate Henry Singleton built. He recruited to the board his
MIT classmate, Claude Shannon, who proved to be an exceptional QS and director.[5] Shannon, who in 1948 pioneered the
development of modern information theory and had a distinguished career as an MIT professor in communications technology, acquired large stakes in Teledyne and a few other companies
he knew well.[6]

Shannon never sold any shares, and by 1981 his portfolio was
composed of the stocks of ten companies, with his Teledyne stake
worth one-third of the total. On the Teledyne board, Shannon
added value due to his depth of technology knowledge, particularly by vetting new acquisitions.

When Singleton retired in 1986, Shannon stepped down too.
Replacing him was Fayez Sarofim, another outstanding QS who
has long held a sizable stake in Teledyne.[7] In recent years, Teledyne's impressive board has included Simon Lorne, a distinguished
figure in the QS ecosystem, who was a former managing partner
of the law firm of Munger, Tolles & Olson, founded by Berkshire
Hathaway's vice chairman, Charlie Munger.

For another recent example, consider the board of AutoNation, led for more than twenty years by CEO Mike Jackson. The
company, owner of a vast network of car dealers, attracted an
impressive list of QSs over those decades.[8] From among these,
two joined the board and were credited by Jackson with vastly
improving corporate performance. Each held 15–16 percent of
the stock for more than a decade: investor Eddie Lampert tutored
board colleagues on capital allocation and Michael Larson of the
Gates Foundation counseled them on disciplined, patient, long-
term thinking.[9]

The board of Credit Acceptance Corporation, lender to sub-
prime borrowers, boasts two distinguished QSs: Scott Vassalluzzo,

of Prescott General Partners, which owns 10 percent of the stock, and Tom Tryforos, who teaches the fundamentals of traditional investing at Columbia Business School. CEO Brett Roberts attests to the enduring value of their board service, stressing in a 2007 letter to shareholders how Tryforos's perspective as an investor helped managers appreciate that all corporate decisions must be tested in terms of a minimum return on capital.

Many other companies adept at attracting QSs have named some to their boards: Berkshire Hathaway in 2005 appointed Sandy Gottesman of First Manhattan, the company's largest shareholder after Warren Buffett since 1966; since going public in 2006, Constellation Software has benefited from the board service of Steve Scotchmer, a distinguished Canadian investor and owner of a large personal stake for decades; and for many years Enstar Group's board included Chuck Akre, a leading QS.

Through 2013 when the Washington Post Co. sold its flagship newspaper, the company had since 1976 saved nearly $1 billion in pension plan costs thanks to savvy investment advice given by the prominent investors Sandy Gottesman and Bill Ruane.[10] Those mavens were suggested and introduced to the company by one of its earliest and most revered QSs: Buffett.[11]

When Fairfax Financial needed expert advice in a valuation matter—CEO Prem Watsa's firm was on the other side of the transaction—it enlisted the services of Sir John Templeton, a large Fairfax shareholder and distinguished QS. Watsa fairly described Templeton as "dean of the investment counselling business." In 2017, Templeton's great-niece, Lauren Templeton, joined the Fairfax board.

As QS Mason Hawkins of Southeastern Asset Management put it when describing how QSs and their investee boards see each other: "Our investment team views our portfolio company management teams and boards of directors as partners, and we engage with them to ensure the greatest value for shareholders over the long term."

Rationality

A share price that is rationally related to business value can be a huge asset for several purposes, including making acquisitions, compensating employees, and facilitating fairly priced gains (or losses) when shareholders must sell. While there is a lively debate over the degree of such market efficiency—of how well price approximates value—companies with the tightest nexus enjoy clear advantages over those with the widest gaps.

Shareholder cohorts have different preferences about the price levels of stocks they own. Transients generally prefer the highest price possible for maximum profit on immediate sale; indexers favor the highest reasonable price because they assume that price and value are substantially the same; and QSs, generally uninterested in an immediate sale and attuned to stock market volatility, prefer a stock price that bears the most rational relationship possible to the company's intrinsic business value.

Many managers tend to likewise prefer the highest possible stock price, perceiving it as a measure of their own performance, the higher the better. But while they often complain that their company's stock price is too low, under- and overpricing are equally likely, and neither is desirable.

Under- and overpricing pose reciprocal problems, such as overpaying or underpaying when using stock as compensation or in acquisitions. Yet at least underpriced shares create value-enhancing corporate opportunities to repurchase shares. Overpricing offers scant offsetting benefits. Worse, it can attract short sellers, a second-best solution to market mispricing, and the bane of corporate managers.

In fact, any perceived benefits—such as an inflated currency to pay colleagues or acquire businesses—soon prove negative when recipients learn the real value of the payment. When an underpriced stock corrects, shareholders cheer the good news. But when an overpriced stock corrects, shareholders detest it, often overreacting with selling pressure that drives price substantially below value.

A spectacular example in recent decades is Dell Inc. from 2002 to 2007.[12] Throughout most of that period, Dell continuously outperformed the broader market. But in mid-2006, shareholders began dumping the stock, and the price plummeted while the market still marched upward.

Rational selling reflected Dell's outdated business model, but downward price pressure prompted further selling amid realization that the stock was substantially overpriced. As investors of many stripes sold the stock, momentum traders followed suit to produce a devastating spiral, erasing all of the gains accumulated over the previous five years.

In the aftermath, employees paid in the inflated shares were furious. Federal authorities determined that the company had stoked the price run-up by massaging earnings to meet the market's inflated expectations.

Another vivid reminder of the hazards of overpriced stock can be seen in the 2000 acquisition by tech upstart America Online (AOL) of media titan Time Warner. Initially hailed as a masterstroke, the much smaller AOL paid $112 billion—in stock—to acquire the entertainment giant. The acquisition soon became a showcase of spectacular failure, however, as AOL was discovered to be worth far less.

A news story on the merger seems written to etch in the memory of chief executives the value of a rational share price:[13] "Now the bitterness and resentment that employees on the Time Warner side have toward their sister division at AOL are straining the company's ability to cooperate, and the restive executives throughout the company have become a vocal stand-in for the company's unhappy shareholders." The chief executives who spearheaded the AOL–Time Warner deal were Gerald Levin and Stephen Case. In the fallout of the overpriced stock deal, both resigned, their reputations stained.

Long-standing empirical research has generally found that inclusion in an index drives stock price up.[14] This occurs as a result of supply and demand, as indexers buy the stock automatically. This drives price above value. Early evidence showed the increase ranged from 3 percent to 9 percent.[15] Moreover, much of the evidence indicates that this price effect was not temporary. Although recent research suggests the effects have diminished over time and on more prominent indexes,[16] permanent market distortions remain a factor managers and directors might consider in deciding what levels of indexers are optimal for their companies.[17]

Evidence suggests that companies with ownership dominated by QSs tend to enjoy stock prices that are less volatile and more rationally related to business value.[18] Ben Graham famously called the stock market in the short run a voting machine and in the long run a weighing machine. To update that insight, *voting* today is principally done by indexers and transients, while *weighing* is the contribution of the QS.

Strategy

Among prominent contemporary competitive advantages are network effects. These arise when a system's value increases as more people use it. In most cases, network effects represent a tangible benefit to customers, as with fax machines in the old days and social media today. An auction site, such as eBay, is a salient example of a business benefiting from network effects. More sellers offering products attract more buyers, which entices more sellers and so on in a compounding circle.

Similar advantages can arise from a network of QSs. As a group, QSs are more likely than others to care about the identity of fellow shareholders. The more QSs a company has the more QSs it is likely to attract. Companies can tap into the broader QS ecosystem, where members tend to know one another or know of one another. QSs bump into each other at shareholder meetings, investor conferences, and other gatherings that focus on the philosophy of concentrated long-term investing. For companies, resulting network effects reinforce all the other advantages of a high-density QS base.

Consumer brands are competitive advantages when they assure customer appreciation and recognition of the quality of the related products.[19] A corporate reputation that attracts QSs is a competitive advantage when a company repeatedly commits to the values long-term committed shareholders appreciate.

Many companies have successfully cultivated reputations among both consumers and shareholders. Take Harley-Davidson, whose shareholders ride their "hogs" in caravans to the annual meeting; Churchill Downs, whose shareholders enjoy many racing days throughout the year and enthusiastic turnouts on Kentucky Derby day; and assorted companies whose brands and owners focus on particular sustainability commitments, such as Patagonia—and more famously, Ben & Jerry's.

There is also a strong association between managers regarded as the best stewards of great brands and QS density rankings. Among U.S. managers ranked in the global elite for brand guardianship, a total of thirty-eight executives, all but one rank in the top half of attracting QSs.[20] Table 3.1 lists a sampling of a dozen select leaders on the combined list.

Because virtually every company makes acquisitions, advantages in the acquisitions market can be a huge source of economic

Table 3.1
Branding and QS density

Amazon	FedEx	P&G
Cisco	Home Depot	UnitedHealth Group
Disney	IBM	Visa
Estée Lauder	Johnson & Johnson	Walmart

value. While most business sellers simply seek top dollar when selling, certain sellers also appreciate intangible values that can tip the scale, at least when the bidding is close.

Companies can obtain an advantage for business acquisitions by cultivating a reputation for honoring permanent commitments. Berkshire Hathaway is famous for doing so, and dozens of other companies follow suit, especially other insurance companies growing merchant investment divisions. While such a reputation may spread by word of mouth from previous sellers, it can be amplified by pointing to a large group of QSs who support the permanent approach. Berkshire and such other companies have sustained their moats in both these ways.

Succession

When a strong chief executive vacates the role, the vacuum can create uncertainty among shareholders as well as employees and customers. Investors may become restless and impatient, causing stock price volatility. QSs support managers through succession, which often takes time, entails bumps, and requires steady commitment to succeed.

When it comes to QSs and management succession, a virtuous circle appears: a high density of QSs can help companies manage succession better, and companies managing succession better attract a higher density of QSs. Two corporate succession stories will illustrate.

In 1991, Don Graham took the helm of the Washington Post Co., succeeding his mother, Kay, who had successfully attracted a sizable cohort of QSs, including Buffett's Berkshire Hathaway. Over ensuing decades, the younger Graham succeeded in retaining and expanding the QS cohort. As of 2005, QSs holding large stakes in the company included a "who's who" of the QS cohort: Berkshire Hathaway, Davis Selected Advisers, First Manhattan,

Franklin Resources, Gardner, Russo & Gardner, Harris Associates (Oakmark Funds), Horizon Kinetics, Klingenstein Fields, Markel Corporation, Massachusetts Financial, and Ruane Cunniff.

As the new century got underway, however, the company faced steadily deteriorating economics: fighting a losing battle for its flagship print newspaper to digital and Internet rivals while defending against intense political attack of its for-profit education business. Seeing weakening economic moats, some of the company's QSs began to withdraw, while others expressed concern.

During this period of adversity, the company sold the *Washington Post* newspaper business, along with another venerable print classic, *Newsweek* magazine. It then divested its banner television station, by swapping it to Berkshire Hathaway in exchange for WaPo stock. It proceeded to spin off its major cable subsidiary, Cable One, and ultimately shrank its for-profit education business through a joint venture with Purdue University. The process spanned four years and ultimately ended with a name change to Graham Holdings Co. (GHC), a much smaller firm.

Amid these substantial changes in both the company's business and its shareholder base, Graham and the board moved forward on succession. First, Graham assumed the role of nonexecutive chairman. As successor, the board appointed his son-in-law, Tim O'Shaughnessy, a 33-year-old online marketing entrepreneur.

The company Graham had led was a very different company than the one O'Shaughnessy took over. Gone were the flagship media properties and substantial education businesses; continuing were far smaller but more agile and tech-oriented ones. Graham wrote to shareholders in 2014, detailing the momentous changes in both the business and his and O'Shaughnessy's contributions. He added:

But the Graham and O'Shaughnessy families are alike in one way: we're heavily concentrated in GHC stock—in my case, it's well over 90 percent of my family's assets. We want to make the stock more valuable for us and for you, our shareholders/part-ners. Our outlook will be long term. Tim's investment focuses will be different from mine. But one thing we share is a long-term orientation.

Today, GHC boasts sizable ownership stakes by such QSs as Fiduciary Management, Southeastern, and Wallace Capital. The moral of this story is the virtuous circle: QSs helped GHC through its transition, including succession, and their continued support has helped GHC ever since.

For a second dramatic succession story, turn to Leucadia National Corporation, a venerable attractor of QSs led for decades by Ian Cumming and Joe Steinberg. By 2010, after a run dating to 1978, the two began considering succession. As they scouted for alternatives, they identified a promising plan in their corporate backyard, so to speak.

Leucadia had a long-term relationship with Jefferies, the invest-ment bank, including professional friendships with its leaders, Rich Handler and Brian Friedman. Although their businesses operated in different sectors, there was some overlap, and the gentlemen all saw eye to eye on fundamentals such as capital allocation and share-holder stewardship. The succession plan involved tectonic shifts: merging Leucadia and Jefferies, installing the Leucadia veterans on the board, and vesting executive offices in the Jefferies team.

Jefferies is a rising investment banking firm, with a vastly dif-ferent culture than the diversified holding company that was Leucadia. When the merger was first announced, press reports and analysts were sour on the move, citing the clash of business models. Many QSs of Leucadia sold their stakes, some within a year or two, including Akre Capital and Markel Corporation; oth-ers steadily sold within the next few years, including Fairholme, Third Avenue, and Tweedy, Browne.

On the other hand, some stalwarts held on, though trim-ming stakes, such as Beck, Mack & Oliver (7.7 million down to

1.7 million) and First Manhattan (6.6 million down to 2.1 million). Others even added to their positions—including Burgundy, Boston Partners, and Mraz Amerine—and still other QSs have been attracted in the years since the merger, including Baillie Gifford, Barrow Hanley, and First Pacific.

Leucadia's selling shareholders appeared to be averse to ownership of a large Wall Street investment bank. Such banks often conceal financial risk exposure during booms, leaving the door open to it being revealed inopportunely during busts. But some perceived this to be an overreaction, as the economics and even the culture would prove attractive to QSs.

For one, Jefferies performed well under CEO Rich Handler, boasting a 14.2 percent compound annual growth rate in book value per share from 1990 to 2012—a span encompassing several market cycles. Reasons included features rare among the investment banking sector: modest leverage, even in the years ahead of the credit crisis when rivals went wild, and high-quality assets, mostly exchange-traded rather than mark-to-model.

Cumming and Steinberg made the judgment that Jefferies was the best home for their lifetime creation. The relative success of their plan is attributable to a considerable degree to the high density of QSs they spent their careers attracting to Leucadia. As Jim Collins made clear in his 1991 classic, *Good to Great*, great managers set up their companies for success after they have left the scene. Aside from tapping a particular person, cultivating a critical mass of QSs should be a high priority.

Now that we have established the advantages—both competitive and comparative—QSs offer, the next part discusses the best ways to attract and communicate with them.

PART II

Quality Engagement

THIS PART DISCUSSES STRATEGIES OF shareholder engagement attractive to QSs. Several seem obvious yet are surprisingly overlooked; others may involve a more conscientious commitment.

Among easy steps any company can take at low cost but few do: corporate mission statements, annual shareholder letters, and annual shareholder meetings. All three are staples of corporate life. Yet many managers see these engagement features as mere incantation, ritual, or regulatory mandate; they are ignored by virtually all indexers, most transients, and some activists. But savvy managers appreciate them as fruitful vehicles to engage QSs. These managers encapsulate the corporate personality in a mission statement; share insights on challenges with a thoughtful annual letter; and reflect on both mission and challenges together at an engaging annual meeting.

Among strategies requiring greater commitment is bucking the tide to abstain from quarterly earnings guidance and conference calls in favor of a longer-term focus. By stopping this habit and breaking the cycle, managers will disappoint transients and attract

QSs. A related step is to adopt, publish, and discuss honest long-term performance metrics, such as economic profit and return on invested capital, in lieu of popular fixations, such as earnings per share. Track these not by quarter or year but over a management team's tenure or company's life, even if that means decades of cumulative comparative data. Such steps will likewise repel transients and attract QSs.

Above all, make a conscious commitment to what QSs value most: effective capital allocation. This refers to a simple but elusive idea that treats every corporate dollar as an investment put to its best use, whether organic or acquired growth, debt reduction, dividends, or share buybacks. Finally, and related, be prepared to rearrange corporate assets, and the equity they represent, through transactions designed to enable businesses to realize their potential value, such as through tracking stocks and spin-offs. These steps can redirect transient shareholders, liberate companies from the indexes and indexers, and deter activist interest.

4

The Corporate Message

INDRA NOOYI, CEO OF PEPSICO from 2006 until 2018, believed in "doing better by doing better." When she was elevated to CEO, she introduced a new motto for the company: "Performance with Purpose." She argued that, for PepsiCo, a snacks and beverage behemoth, financial success and social responsibility were inextricably linked. Nooyi deftly tapped into a zeitgeist of the times, one prevalent not only in the shareholder demographic, but pervasive in the labor markets from which PepsiCo draws its talent and among its principal customer base. Appreciating how so many young adults care about the environment and sustainability, PepsiCo had to as well. Nooyi wrote:

> The Performance with Purpose means delivering sustainable growth by investing in a healthier future for people and our planet. . . . We will continue to build a portfolio of enjoyable and healthier foods and beverages, find innovative ways to reduce the use of energy, water, and packaging, and provide a great

workplace for our associates. . . . Because a healthier future for all people and our planet means a more successful future for PepsiCo. This is our promise.

Nooyi succeeded in getting the PepsiCo motto heard as she touted the "Performance with Purpose" motto in public appearances and interviews alike.

Corporate messages can be communicated in multiple ways. Certain companies adopt succinct mission statements, others bullet-point owner's manuals. Many enshrine their messages early in their lives, while others get around to it later. Companies publish clear formal statements on their websites or just let the message percolate organically through shareholder letters or annual reports. While the medium can vary, the content is vital. And that content is the starting point for a strategy of cultivating QSs.

A Sampling of Messages

A few rules of thumb for the corporate message. Make sure that it suits the company and is distinctive. Make sure it is honest and true. Make sure it sends the right message to all stakeholders— from employees to customers to shareholders.

In an effort to provide shareholders a menu for Berkshire Hathaway, Buffett created an owner's manual, with fifteen short propositions.[1] A substantial, clear, and comprehensive guide, these subjects include many of the perspectives that appeal to QSs, including long-term goals and a desire for rational share pricing. A selection from this manual:

- Although our form is corporate, our attitude is partnership.
- In line with Berkshire's owner-orientation, most of our directors have a major portion of their net worth invested in the company.

- Our long-term economic goal is to maximize Berkshire's average annual rate of gain in intrinsic business value on a per-share basis.
- Accounting consequences do not influence our operating or capital-allocation decisions.
- We test the wisdom of retaining earnings by assessing whether retention, over time, delivers shareholders at least $1 of market value for each $1 retained.
- We will be candid in our reporting to you, emphasizing the pluses and minuses important in appraising business value.

Some companies have adopted credos that continue to withstand the test of time. Among the most durable and famous is that of Johnson & Johnson (J&J). Written personally by the longtime chairman and member of the founding family, Robert Wood Johnson, the credo has remained the same since 1943 when the company went public.

What's most notable in the J&J credo is the hierarchy of priorities: customers, employees, communities, and then stockholders.[2] The philosophy stresses doing well by doing good: doing good on behalf of the other constituencies is the path to doing well for shareholders. It's a statement of values that precedes ensuing cries for corporate social responsibility and today's environmental, social, and governance proponents.

J&J's classic credo was the model for such a statement adopted in 2019 by the Business Roundtable, a leading group of chief executives of large U.S. companies.[3] There is strong association between those signatory companies and QS density, suggesting a strong association between the commitment expressed in the mission statement and attracting QSs.[4]

To see how doing well by customers and employees entails doing well by shareholders, consider the example of health-care products distributor Henry Schein Inc. Under the stewardship of Stanley Bergman, shareholder returns have outperformed peers and the broader market since the company went public in 1995. Bergman explains:

> For the suppliers, the customers and the teams to work together, you need capital, because it's a business. We are very clear with Wall Street: Henry Schein does not exist for the investors. Having said that, we promise the investors a good rate of return and we deliver on those expectations. It's not the greatest return, it's not a bad return, it's consistent. We've been public for 19 years and in that 19 years, we've grown the earnings each year by about 16 percent [on average].

Other companies simply cut to the chase, stressing a goal of assuring maximal shareholder value. That direct approach is epitomized in the following statement of corporate mission—by a venerable attractor of QSs:

> Our primary objective will continue to be the maximization of shareholder value. We will manage our business to generate earnings growth and improved returns. We plan to reinvest a greater portion of our resources in projects and investments that strategically augment and leverage our operations—investments where the long-term cash returns on invested capital exceed our overall cost of capital.

Written in 1984 by Roberto Goizueta, chairman of the Coca-Cola Company, that statement of corporate objective appealed to QSs. One of those was Warren Buffett, whose Berkshire Hathaway loaded up on the stock in 1988, added more over ensuing years, and still holds all that stock to this day.

A mission statement might appeal specifically to the competitive advantages of a high density of QSs, such as promoting a rational share price. That's one bullet in the 270-word, seven-point mission statement of AMERCO, also known as U-Haul. They are presented in the 2004 shareholder letter by CEO Joe Shoen, who takes a pithy, no-nonsense approach to running the company in which his family has long owned a substantial stake. The mission statement includes the following, with stock price rationality referenced last:

- Operating in a specialty niche, where our success is dependent more on how we treat our customers than on competitive or market conditions.
- Developing a self-funding balance sheet. Expand by using our own profits.
- Maintaining substantial insider ownership. This includes Shoen interests, ESOP and individual ownership by directors, employees, dealers and vendors.
- Maintaining constructive labor relations. Management free to make decisions independent of outside groups. Encourage a coincidence of interest between ownership, management, operative U-Haul System members and dealers.
- Maintaining a reasonable price/earnings ratio on our common stock. Emphasize the strength of the company, not the strength of the stock price.

For executives feeling undecided over whether to express principles formally or leave norms to develop informally, consider a page from Prem Watsa, head of Fairfax Financial, the Toronto-based insurance company. At Fairfax, formal guidelines had been adopted internally and circulated for a decade before being released publicly. Here are selections from the Fairfax principles, which Watsa has appended to his annual shareholder letter for two decades, stressing that they remain intact:

Objectives. Our focus is long term growth in book value per share and not quarterly earnings. We plan to grow through internal means as well as through friendly acquisitions.

Structure. Our companies are decentralized and run by the presidents except for performance evaluation, succession planning, acquisitions, financing and investments, which are done by or with Fairfax. Investing will always be conducted based on a long-term value-oriented philosophy. Share ownership and large incentives are encouraged across the Group.

Values. We always look at opportunities but emphasize downside protection and look for ways to minimize loss of capital. We are entrepreneurial. We encourage calculated risk taking. It is all right to fail but we should learn from our mistakes. We will never bet the company on any project or acquisition. We believe in having fun—at work!

For companies with multiple divisions, a further option is letting each division decide whether to adopt formal statements and exactly how. That's the approach at Constellation Software, whose nearly four hundred separate vertical market software businesses are run through six operating groups. One group states its

Table 4.1
Weak mission statements

"To be the best in the eyes of our customers, employees and shareholders."
"Profitable growth through superior customer service, innovation, quality and commitment."
"We strive to be the acknowledged global leader and preferred partner in helping our clients succeed in the world's rapidly evolving financial markets."
"To maximize long-term stockholder value, while obeying the law and observing the highest ethical standards."
"Undisputed market leadership."
"To supply outstanding service and solutions through dedication and excellence."
"We will continue to build a corporate culture that respects and values the unique strengths and cultural differences of our associates."

Table 4.2
Strong mission statements

"To bring inspiration and innovation to every athlete in the world. If you have a body, you are an athlete."—Nike (stresses product effects on customer experience)
"Helping people on their path to better health."—CVS (credible from the chain that ceased selling cigarettes, despite profitability)
"Creating happiness through magical experiences."—Walt Disney (employees and shareholders alike love this, and it's true)
"To be a company that inspires and fulfills your curiosity."—Sony (inspired)
"To make our cars better, our employees happier and our planet a better place to be."—Ford Motor Co. (almost sounds like Henry Ford speaking to rally his start-up)
"We fulfill dreams of personal freedom."—Harley-Davidson (evokes the product and customer experience)
"We're in business to save our home planet."—Patagonia (more famous for its environmental commitment than for its outdoor equipment)

manager's top ten rules, another uses an emblem of ten values in its logo, while others have nothing of the sort.

Clever rhetoric and empty slogans are ineffective in mission statements. Equally unhelpful are general aspirations shared by rivals—they fail to stand out. Tables 4.1 and 4.2 present some examples of both weak and strong mission statements.[5] As it happens, the strong examples are from companies ranking high for QS density.[6]

Indexer Demands Versus QS Appeals

Index funds buy all stocks in an index without regard to mission statement or any other particular feature of a company. That has not stopped major indexers from demanding that companies produce them. For instance, BlackRock, the massive indexer, in a

2016 open letter to chief executives, requested companies to adopt statements. The indexer expressed special interest in having companies explain how corporate mission relates to social interests. Many did so in response.

One was Alleghany Corporation, founded in 1929, which in 2017 published a baker's dozen of propositions. These explain what the company does, primarily writing insurance—and its social values—including spreading risk, all in a brisk 780 words.

Ironically, while inspired by an indexing behemoth with little interest in individual companies, the Alleghany statement is an impressive appeal to QSs. Its statement of values and practices includes several discussed later in this book that attract QSs.

- Alleghany was originally a family-owned business. Although this is no longer the case, that legacy remains an essential part of our culture and is important to how we conduct ourselves. We expect our executives and managers to treat employees fairly and equitably, and to be responsible to the communities in which they operate and the constituencies that they serve. And we endeavor to custody shareholder capital as if it were our own.
- As the owner of insurance and reinsurance companies, Alleghany Corporation itself is, to a significant degree, an asset management company. Like a closed-end fund, the corporation retains most of its profits and reinvests those profits on behalf of its stockholders.
- Alleghany Capital Corporation is our investment subsidiary that acquires and oversees primarily non-financial companies with durable businesses. Unlike a private equity firm, we do not acquire companies with the intention to sell them in the future. Rather, we believe that we provide a stable ownership structure when the founders or other control owners need to effect a capital transition. We believe that our ownership allows our owner-manager

partners to grow their company and to improve each company's results over time.

- Our primary function in overseeing operating businesses is to provide strategic guidance, to set risk parameters, and to ensure that management incentives are appropriate. We don't "run" our subsidiaries—their executive teams do.
- We do not provide financial guidance, and do not hold quarterly earnings conference calls.

While BlackRock and other indexers may request mission statements, despite such statements having no effect on their investment decisions, QSs routinely publish statements about what they are looking for in their investments. Managers writing corporate menus should consider these statements of shareholder appetite in serving up their offerings. Consider the following sampling from Cedar Rock, Gardner, Russo & Gardner, and Southeastern Asset Management.

Cedar Rock Capital Partners

Our investment approach is to buy and hold shares in companies that we believe capable of compounding in value over the long term. Our investment criteria emphasize quality, value and managerial character. We define high-quality businesses as being capable of sustaining high returns on their operating capital employed without requiring financial leverage, and of reinvesting at least a portion of their excess cash flows at high rates of return. We consider such companies to be attractively valued when their normalized excess cash flows, calculated as a percentage of the companies' equity market capitalizations, compare favorably with long-term interest rates.

We devote much of our research effort to assessing corporate managers for their probity, trustworthiness and ability to reinvest their corporate cash flows at attractive rates of returns for shareholders. Our criteria are demanding and our portfolios tend to be concentrated in approximately 20 companies, selected globally. We make no effort to minimize volatility relative to any national, regional or global index of equity market performance. However, we expect our emphasis on both quality and value to generate satisfactory absolute and relative performance over the long term.

Gardner, Russo & Gardner

To merit our investing attention a company must possess unique characteristics. Its businesses' competitive advantages must give indication of stability and growth. This is measured by its sustainable long-term returns on capital and by consistent generation of free cash flow. The company must be run by a management team with a proven record of successful operation and effective allocation of free cash flow.

It must also possess the type of firm culture that provides the context and incentive for long-term value creation. This means a management that brings the most effective of "family-owned" approaches to running their operations (long-term wealth-building rather than short-term profit-harvesting; interest in proactively maintaining reputational value of a business; deep knowledge of its businesses and of the industry in which its businesses operate).

We look to invest in companies which have the "capacity to reinvest" that are run by shareholder-minded managements who have the "capacity to suffer" Wall Street disapproval while directing heavy investments intended to generate future growth but which all-too-often adversely impact near-term reported profits.

Southeastern Asset Management

We invest in strong businesses that are understandable, financially sound, competitively positioned, and have ample free cash flow that may grow over time. These businesses are run by good people—honorable and trustworthy, highly skilled operators and capital allocators, who are focused on building value per share and have incentives aligned with their shareholders.

We seek to take advantage of short-term market emotions. We are long-term owners, not traders or speculators, and invest for the long-term based on objective intrinsic values with a horizon of at least five years.

We construct our portfolios with what we believe to be our best 18–22 global investment ideas. Concentrating allows for adequate diversification while providing some of the best opportunities to maximize returns, and minimize loss of principal.

Our investment team views our portfolio company management teams and boards of directors as partners, and we engage with them to ensure the greatest value for shareholders over the long term.

The corporate message is just one method of outreach to QSs. Another is the annual letter, referenced multiple times in this chapter, and discussed explicitly in chapter 5.

5

Annual Letters

DEAR SHAREHOLDER:

Recently, a head coach made a seemingly counterintuitive statement be-fore a game when he said, "I think that the team that makes the most mistakes will win." That sounded like an unusual statement, but he went on to say that his team needed to be aggressive, and be willing to make mistakes, to produce a victory.

An unhealthy fear of mistakes can lead to being too passive or fearful. That leads to stiffness and subpar results. It is important to be willing to act positively, and accept reasonable mistakes, so that the organization can learn, and grow, and deal with a rapidly changing world.

We do that at Markel, and we think that this willingness to take per-sonal responsibility, admit errors, learn, and move forward is a unique competitive advantage for the company.

Tom Gayner et al. (2012)

DEAR SHAREHOLDER:

Last year one of America's icons, Yogi Berra, passed away. As a tribute I have sprinkled some of his better-known witticisms throughout the letter and will sign off with one of his most frequently quoted quips, "It 'ain't' over till it's over."

SEACOR had a terrible year in 2015. As of today, 2016 doesn't look much better, but we step to the "plate" with an excellent bat, our strong balance sheet. We are waiting for a "fat pitch." If necessary to protect our balance sheet, we will step out of the batter's box.

Charles Fabrikant (2015)

As these sample passages show, an artfully drafted shareholder letter provides insights into a company's values, culture, and outlook. It is the forum of greatest freedom for CEO expression, as the letter is both optional and unregulated. It is therefore the ideal place for the CEO to convey both individual and corporate personality. CEOs reassure current shareholders by reiterating corporate values, reintroducing management personalities, and reflecting the corporate trajectory. These communications are an excellent tool in attracting QSs.

Elements

One reason the shareholder letter provides an excellent way to cultivate quality is that so many CEOs simply don't bother with them—those who try have an automatic competitive advantage. Even across companies offering such letters, only a minority of companies archive them on their websites. Analysts who have read large samplings among letters that are accessible attest that only a handful are worth reading—fewer than 3 percent by one estimate.[1]

Scan surveys of the best shareholder letters—either a search of published materials or a poll at an investor gathering—and the same names keep coming up. Observers, however, give high marks to shareholder letters for different reasons.

For example, many rankings of the "best" shareholder letters score general clarity; some run algorithms searching for linguistic cues across the continuum from candid to obfuscating.[2]

Some investors view shareholder letters as a screen to sort out prospective investments and to supplement more typical analytical filters.[3]

Clarity and candor are virtues. It is best to be upfront about challenges facing the company. Substance and style both matter. Laura Rittenhouse, founder of Rittenhouse Rankings, which analyzes shareholder letters, offers this advice on what to avoid: "platitudes, clichés, corporate jargon, and confusing statements that lack important context." Warren Buffett's pithy statement from his 1997 letter put it well:

> When you receive a communication from us, it will come from the fellow you are paying to run the business. Your Chairman has a firm belief that owners are entitled to hear directly from the CEO as to what is going on and how he evaluates the business, currently and prospectively. You would demand that in a private company; you should expect no less in a public company.

Single letters taken in isolation are less meaningful than an arc over many years. Quite a few CEOs have written one great letter, but the best keep it up year after year. Studying the letters of a large number of companies over a long period of time yields valuable guidance for shareholders and managers alike. Having culled the archives, I collected the best of the genre in the book *Dear Shareholder*, presenting seventeen different companies, all adept at attracting QSs.

A common theme: growing into the letters. The best letters are those of the experienced leader—outstanding executives tend to develop in the job and get better with engagement. CEOs should not get discouraged: writing shareholder letters can be difficult at first, but it tends to get easier with passing years.

On the other hand, sometimes the first letter turns out great. Jeff Bezos's most effective letter, from the standpoint of attracting QSs, was his first in 1997. It is so good he appended it to every

ensuing annual letter to Amazon shareholders. That keeps the letter on message while enabling Bezos to discuss product develop-
ments, Amazon culture, and his own distinctive philosophies on
business and life.

Many CEOs find support in the letter writing from other members of their team. For example, at Leucadia in the early years, the
top executives, Ian Cumming and Joe Steinberg, wrote magnificent
shareholder letters with a broad assessment of corporate affairs.
They then attached separate detailed commentary on specific operations from the heads of various units. At Fairfax Financial in the
early going, chairman Prem Watsa enclosed a separate letter from
the company's chief insurance manager for detailed discussion of
that business.

Some CEOs share the burdens and joys of letter writing with colleagues. Kay Graham, the legendary leader of the Washington Post
Co. from the 1970s through the 1990s—which famously attracted
very high-quality shareholders, including Buffett—almost always
shared the signature line with one or more colleagues. At Markel,
the letter has almost always had multiple authors—in one recent
installation they signed off as "The Band."

Yet others have gained inspiration by making their letters into
a company pitch. They target not only QSs but outline acquisition
criteria and even advertise the company's products. Leucadia ran
humorous annual spots boosting its vineyards in the early 2000s,
with such whimsical hyperbole as this: "One glass each day of
Pine Ridge or Archery Summit wine extends life and makes your
fellow shareholders happy."

Marketers are big on testimonials, and they can have a place in
the shareholder letter, when done well. Consider this endorsement
from the 2006 letter to shareholders of Morningstar, the financial
information company:

> We offer a unique product. When people try it, they like it—
> whether they're small investors or well-known money managers.

I received a letter from Sir John Templeton, one of the preeminent investors of our time, saying he found our equity research to be "top quality." That's the type of feedback that tells us we're doing something right.

Warren Buffett's letters are famous for this practice. On many occasions, Buffett first commented on the performance of Berkshire's Geico car insurance subsidiary, then inserted an unabashed ad, as in 2015 when the discussion concluded: "Indeed, at least 40 percent of the people reading this letter can save money by insuring with GEICO. So stop reading—right now!—and go to geico.com or call 800-368-2734."

As an additional opportunity, there is no better place than the shareholder letter to include a pitch to prospective business partners and sellers. Buffett has done this famously for decades, stating Berkshire's acquisition criteria and asking for referrals.

The practice has been followed widely, including in Don Graham's 2002 Washington Post Co. letter ("[Our] Company is a good home for well-run media and education businesses that have a special character and want to keep it") and Markel's 2010 missive ("We offer tremendous advantages to potential sellers of these businesses. . . . P.S. If you or someone you know owns a business that meets these criteria and would like to find a permanent home let us know.")

Another feature of outstanding letters is originality, reflecting the personality of the writer and culture of the company. QSs know the difference between legitimate emulation and mindless copycatting. The best letters—as with any kind of writing—are those written with sincerity and passion.

Above all, the golden rule of shareholder letters: Buffett says he writes to provide shareholders information he would want to have if their "positions were reversed." Markel's 2017 letter opens with a similar invocation, stating the writers' goal as providing everything "we would want to know about Markel if our roles were reversed."

A degree of repetition is valuable—especially on enduring core values and practices. One endearing feature of many letters for QSs is core principles that do not change. Such a firm belief system is valuable to QSs—whatever happens in the world, they know the company stays true to its values. Such statements are therefore worthy of repetition.

Consistency is a virtue, especially in presenting figures and charts. Ideally, letters use the same measures and graphs to analyze performance over the years. As data lovers, QSs appreciate substantial historical figures. Many shareholder letters feature such information, at least a decade, some going back multiple decades (Alleghany, Credit Acceptance, Markel, SEACOR); one half a century (Berkshire); and one nearly a century (Genuine Parts Company, from 1928). As one QS, Mark Hughes of Lafayette Investments, observed about Genuine Parts: "When you show 90 years of results, the picture is clear that this is an enduring business with a long-term focus."[4]

When authors introduce new metrics and charts, they should explain their utility. If omitting data in one year that appeared previously, the writer must explain why. Readers who need to hunt to see whether goalposts have changed may instead change their views on the company's appeal.

The shareholder letters by Brett Roberts of Credit Acceptance Corporation are a model of consistency. For nearly two decades, each letter has followed an almost identical format, with several tables and charts appearing throughout in the same order. This approach makes it easy for first-time readers and veterans alike to gain a complete, consistent picture of the business and its performance.

Consider the following paragraph appearing in virtually identical form at the top of Credit Acceptance Corporation's annual shareholder letters year after year. The only changes from 2007 to 2017 are the numbers of years elapsed (35 to 45) and lives changed (thousands to millions):

> Our core product has remained essentially unchanged for 45 years. We provide auto loans to consumers regardless of their credit history. Our customers consist of individuals who have typically been turned away by other lenders. Traditional lenders have many reasons for declining a loan. We have always believed that a significant number of individuals, if given an opportunity to establish or reestablish a positive credit history, will take advantage of it. As a result of this belief, we have changed the lives of millions of people.

Finally, save fawning for employee pep rallies. Focus shareholder letters on challenges, not triumphs. Phil Carret, a legendary investor, though more inclined to diversify than most QSs, gave good advice based on his studious reading of shareholder letters: "I'm always turned off by an overly optimistic letter from the president in the annual report. If [the] letter is mildly pessimistic, to me that's a good sign. I like a point I once heard made by a corporate chief executive, that he was less interested in hearing good news from subordinates than bad news. The good news takes care of itself."[5]

Examples

In short, the annual shareholder letter is one of the most successful means QSs and managers use to connect with each other. To illustrate the mutual value of such letters to both cohorts, my book *Dear Shareholder* showcases exemplary selections from this genre; the companies and authors are listed in table 5.1.

Many distinguished QSs and authors expressed their appreciation of such outstanding shareholder letters in assessing this

Table 5.1
Shareholder letters and QS density

Alleghany: Weston Hicks	Graham Holdings (WaPo): Don Graham
Amazon: Jeff Bezos	IBM: Virginia Rometty
Berkshire Hathaway: Warren Buffett	Jefferies: Rich Handler and Brian Friedman
Cimpress: Robert Keane	Leucadia: Ian Cumming and Joe Steinberg
Coca-Cola: Roberto Goizueta	Markel Corporation: Tom Gayner
Constellation Software: Mark Leonard	Morningstar: Joe Mansueto
Credit Acceptance: Brett Roberts	PepsiCo: Indra Nooyi
Fairfax Financial: Prem Watsa	SEACOR: Charles Fabrikant
Google: Larry Page and Sergey Brin	

collection. Howard Marks observed: "Little has been written about CEOs' letters to shareholders." The best letters illustrate "what makes for a successful company and a great CEO." Will Thorndike, author of a QS bible, *The Outsiders*, declared that the best letters are "a treasure trove" for investors and managers alike, especially when the message resonates with topics of great importance to QSs, such as a shareholder orientation and an appreciation of the fundamentals of capital allocation. Lauren Templeton, niece of the late Sir John Templeton, finds "invaluable lessons and insights" in the best shareholder letters.

The audience is substantial, intelligent, and appreciative. Professor George Athanassakos, the Ben Graham Chair in Value Investing, Ivey School of Business, University of Western Ontario, says that the best shareholder letters reflect certain values, especially "integrity, humility, discipline, patience, and long-term perspective." Another student of the genre, Jeff Gramm, author of *Dear Chairman*, says the best shareholder letters "teach us

Table 5.2
Rittenhouse rankings and QS density

ADP	CVS	Microsoft
Amazon.com	Edison International	Netflix
Becton, Dickinson	General Mills	Sherwin-Williams
Charles Schwab	General Motors	Southwest Airlines
Clorox	Google	Texas Instruments
Costco	Honeywell	Travelers
	Lockheed Martin	

valuable lessons about management, leadership and corporate stewardship." And Jake Taylor, noted author of *The Rebel Allocator*, notes that "shareholder letters are a unique keyhole into the business world."

One expert on the shareholder letter, Laura Rittenhouse, stresses that reading the best letters can "boost your strategic IQ and your investment returns." In a recent annual ranking, Rittenhouse designated the top 25 by her measures, the vast majority of which rank among the highest in terms of attracting QSs. Table 5.2 lists these companies.[6]

One last point on annual letters: companies and shareholders can get the most bang for their buck when the letter is tied into the annual meeting, discussed in chapter 6.

6

Annual Meetings

"*THIS* MEETING IS VERY DIFFERENT!" exclaimed Ingrid Hendershot, a QS, attending the Tootsie Roll annual shareholders meeting.[1] Her attention was riveted on the front of the room, where Mel Gordon, the company's octogenarian chairman and CEO, and his septuagenarian wife, Ellen, president and COO, took the stage. Mel ran through the agenda and Ellen described new products, pulling out boxes and boxes of candy that circulated the room.

With a history dating to 1896 and annual sales of $540 million, Tootsie Roll's brands include its namesake oblong chocolate roll along with Charleston Chew, Junior Mints, and Sugar Daddy. Ellen spoke of the candy's new packaging, handed out more samples, and fielded questions. After one shareholder pressed her on how trends favoring healthy foods could adversely affect the company, she acknowledged the possibility, but quipped: "We believe strongly that candy and treats are a logical part of a healthy diet."

Hendershot says the meeting is candid and folksy without "sugarcoating," as another shareholder quipped, comparing it favorably to the famous Berkshire Hathaway annual meeting.

Also striking about the Tootsie Roll meeting is how the Gordon family and leadership of Tootsie Roll run a public company but are reclusive people. Tootsie Roll headquarters has been likened to Willie Wonka's mythic chocolate factory, surrounded by fences and a veil of secrecy. The shareholder meeting is therefore one of the few opportunities to get to know them, ask questions, and engage with management. And of course, gorge on candy.

At most companies, the annual meeting is a perfunctory affair, with a two-hour meeting considered lengthy.[2] While time is usually allotted for shareholder questions, the "questions" often seem more like pet peeves than probes of company strategy and prospects. Those responding tend to focus narrowly or literally on the particular questions, rather than listening for clues about wider shareholder concerns that create opportunities to educate shareholders about the company's strategy and prospects.

But it doesn't have to be that way, and scores of companies buck the boring approach. They offer videos, product samples, lengthy Q&As, educational programs, and more. In a few cases, additional events surround the meeting, such as separate meetings of major subsidiaries or breakout sessions with key managers. As *New Yorker* columnist John Brooks reported, annual meetings "bring companies to life."[3] QSs relish this in-the-flesh opportunity to see the company in action and engage with the personalities. Hosting an engaging annual meeting is a great way to attract and keep QS.

History

Before the 1930s, annual shareholder meetings were perfunctory legal affairs that achieved little and attracted few. Amid rising individual share ownership, a vocal group of gadflies, led by the brothers John and Lewis Gilbert, spent the next four decades making meetings matter.[4]

By the early 1960s across corporate America, up to ten annual meetings drew more than one thousand shareholders; two dozen between three hundred and nine hundred; and AT&T, boasting millions of shareholders, set the era's record at twelve thousand attendees. A 1964 *New York Times* story proclaimed: "The vociferous minority shareholders helped popularize meetings by their persistent attendance and their keen questioning on controversial matters."[5]

In the early 1970s, a movement to abandon the annual meeting flickered fleetingly. In 1972, Delaware, the leading state of incorporation for public companies, updated its law to let shareholders act by written consent rather than at meetings. In a *New York Times* op-ed, J. B. Fuqua, of Fuqua Industries, advocated for abolition, in favor of voting by mail.

But shareholders overwhelmingly pushed back, and stock exchanges ruled that the consent method did not meet their requirement to have an annual meeting. By 1975, the abolition movement was dead, wryly judged by the *New York Times* as "notably unsuccessful."

That same year, Warren Buffett began building what would become the most popular annual shareholder meeting, at Berkshire Hathaway. In 1975, a dozen attended in an Omaha office cafeteria, but then for the next three decades added a digit—hundreds by 1985, thousands by 1995, and tens of thousands by 2005. In 2018, more than forty thousand attended, the record for a U.S. public company.

While the Berkshire meeting's main feature has long been a six-hour Q&A with Buffett and vice chairman Charlie Munger, it has evolved into a weekend-long extravaganza. The company for decades has hosted events on the days surrounding the meeting—a Friday night ball game, Saturday evening cookout, Sunday champagne brunch—and shareholders have added their own conferences, panels, and parties that alone draw hundreds or thousands. As recounted in an edited collection of essays, *The Warren Buffett Shareholder*, it is a series of energetic scenes of engaged QSs.[6]

Markel Corporation hosts an impressive annual meeting in its hometown of Richmond, Virginia—but it also hosts a separate gathering, drawing some thirteen hundred shareholders in Omaha during the weekend of the Berkshire meeting. Detecting overlap in both shareholders and values, CEO Tom Gayner began the tradition in 1985, when he was a junior insurance manager. A half dozen joined him. Gayner has continued to lead the event since. The day after the Berkshire annual meeting, he and colleagues sit on the dais all morning and address questions from an attentive crowd.

Evolution

From 1980 through 2010, ownership of public company equity shifted from individuals to institutions. With that shift, companies increasingly communicated to shareholders throughout the year, always at regular quarterly intervals and often more frequently, approaching a model of continuous disclosure.

While ownership and communication changed, the annual meeting remained a staple of corporate life, an important opportunity for shareholders—both individuals and representatives of institutions—to meet management, pose questions, press issues, and resolve debate.

But if the prior era's annual meetings stressed individual shareholders and associated "democratic" rights, this one increasingly brought out corporate identity and culture. For example, Ben & Jerry's Homemade, from 1984 until its sale to Unilever in 2000, attracted a crew of socially responsible owners to a meeting that looked more like Woodstock than Wall Street.

Held among cattle farms near Burlington, Vermont, the meeting was run informally, the founders weaving in the vocabulary of hippies: Jerry Greenfield, one of the founders, might intone, "Hey, man, time for a little Q&A." If Ben Cohen made a motion, in unison a chorus could be heard paraphrasing Smokey Robinson, singing, "I second that motion."[7]

The company's commitment to sustainable profitability and social responsibility through charitable giving resonated with this group. Pressed by critics on board authority to allocate corporate profits to charitable causes, Ben Cohen, Greenfield's partner, explained:

> We've never taken a formal vote of all the shareholders, but at our annual meetings, I usually ask them—just a show of hands, it's nonbinding—if they support the company's supporting the community and giving away what are really their profits. And they're all in favor of it.

The Ben & Jerry's annual meeting helped to communicate the company's brand, attracting both consumers and like-minded shareholders, forging enduring loyalties. Moreover, it was achieved at low cost and produced high returns.

Another mighty American town, Fayetteville, Arkansas, has been the scene of the Walmart stockholders' meeting, most distinctive because of its conscious focus on employees, many of whom are also shareholders. Founder Sam Walton hosted the first Walmart Stores annual meeting in 1970 at a coffee shop with five other people. Since the 1980s, the meetings have added special events and celebrity guests drawing large crowds. The venue has moved from the headquarters' auditorium to University of Arkansas arenas now seating twenty thousand.

Walmart executives bound onto stage under flashes of light, met with roars of approval from the crowd. Managers get the crowd to spell out "Walmart," declare that the store is "number one," and proclaim their love of the brand. Though Walmart remains an economic powerhouse serving its shareholders well, its identity is in its employees, whom it affectionately calls "associates." The annual meeting is their centerpiece.

Positive reinforcement and mutual admiration are also expressed at the annual meeting of Southeastern Asset Management, where chairman O. Mason Hawkins boasted: "We have the best shareholders in the mutual fund business."[8] Such a claim has rivals, however, such as Ruane Cunniff, which runs the famed Sequoia Fund. It cultivates engaged long-term investors, attracting and retaining them through its annual meetings that draw one thousand every May to New York City.

Fairfax Financial hosts an annual meeting in its hometown of Toronto as well as a separate investor day in New York. The annual meeting likewise started small, but today draws thousands, who gather in a collegial spirit. For nearly a decade, Fairfax has sponsored a value investing conference the day before; booths are staffed by the company's subsidiaries—mostly insurance, but also restaurants and gift shops, as well as educational and cultural institutions the company supports. Prem Watsa devotes a full page of his annual shareholder letter to advertising the attractions.

Highlights

The annual meeting can be a place where shareholders see the human face of a company and its culture. They meet the chairperson, operating and executive teams, and even the board. During his tenure at DuPont, CEO and chairman Chad Holliday would wander up and down the aisles, shaking hands with shareholders in a show of savvy but human leadership.[9] Directors usually attend shareholders meeting and are introduced to the crowd. In some cases, they are asked to play additional roles, from serving as emcee to introducing themselves and giving their backgrounds.

One who has attended hundreds of shareholder meetings, and written a book reviewing them, is Randy Cepuch, who recounts one such story:[10]

At the AGM of Ansell, an Australian company, one year: The entire board enters the room at once. . . . Chairman Dr. Ed Tweddell, . . . introduces his fellow panelists, including several nominees for board seats. I've seen enough such acknowledgements to assume that the nominees will simply stand and nod at the shareholders. But that's not what happens! "Could each of you please tell us a few things about yourselves?" Tweddell asks. And they do, effectively offering campaign speeches even though they're running unopposed. It's a wonderful, refreshing gesture that goes a long way toward humanizing the board and the company.

At some annual meetings, companies offer freebies to shareholders, as at Tootsie Roll. Product samples from Ben & Jerry's ice cream are given out at Unilever meetings, box lunches are served at Marks & Spencer and British Petroleum.[11] These gestures keep those attending happy and entice them to return. Successful shareholder meetings tend to draw more people every year—as a company prospers and word spreads. Shareholder meeting critic Cepuch again:[12]

Chalone's president, Tom Selfridge, "explains that this is the thirty-fifth [annual shareholders' meeting]. The first, held in a kitchen, drew six people and was over in ten minutes—not counting a few hours of wine drinking afterward. Word apparently spread quickly, because two years later there were fifty attendees, and by 1986 more than five hundred shareholders and guests showed up. Selfridge points out that this gathering draws a much bigger crowd than shareholder meetings for many Fortune 500 companies.

Future

Executives who have perfected the practice of the live annual meeting may have a competitive advantage as companies migrate to the virtual approach. Authorization to host virtual-only shareholder meetings was first enacted in 2000 by Delaware corporate law. Today, most state corporate laws permit the practice as well.[13] The pandemic that spread in early 2020 prompted pervasive switch from in-person to virtual meetings, a shift that some forecast would persist post-pandemic.

In the first decade after virtual meetings were authorized, a smattering of smaller companies opted in, led by ICU Medical and Herman Miller. During this period, a few big names publicly evaluated the virtual-only option. Among these, a half dozen opted against doing so after hearing negative feedback from shareholders, while another half dozen went forward, despite negative feedback.

Notably, the companies that went forward tend to enjoy a relatively higher QS density than those pulling back. Among those adhering to live meetings are several in the top quarter in attracting QSs: ConocoPhillips, Symantec, and Union Pacific. Among those that went virtual yet remain adept at attracting QSs: Comcast, Duke Energy, Intel, and PayPal.[14]

For many companies, the answer became to offer both live and virtual meetings—as done by Cisco Systems from 2005 and Berkshire from 2016. But even in compromise, costs and critics remain. Google's live meeting was also streamed and received entirely different reviews from those attending versus those watching. Those in the room reported being energized and engaged, while those live blogging remotely reflected a perception of blandness. Critic Cepuch chalks it up to the sensory difference between being an *eye*witness or merely an *ear*witness.[15]

While each company must make its own assessment based on its situation, a few general arguments on each side should be noted. Proponents cite several advantages for virtual-only shareholder meetings, which opponents counter.

Advantages are lower costs, potentially increasing the number of shareholders tuning in, and a cost–benefit framework that stresses that few attend and little occurs. Opponents counter that such features are not inevitable, as many managers have harnessed the shareholder meeting as a productive forum for all. Poor turnout and banality are the managers' fault and more a sign of a problem to be fixed than a rationale for further dilution, critics say.

Another general argument holds that institutional owners cannot attend all the meetings for companies in which they own stock, because their portfolios are so diversified, and having the ability to tune in increases coverage. This argument may be especially compelling for indexers owning stock in hundreds or thousands of companies without the staff to attend most of them. But this seems more a critique of indexing than of live meetings. In any event, at current staffing levels of indexers, they would not be able to attend a great many meetings, even if all were virtual.

The most compelling argument favoring virtual meetings arose during the pandemic amid the 2020 annual meeting season: there was simply no other way to proceed. But the experience during the pandemic otherwise cut both ways, ultimately amplifying the arguments on both sides.

No matter which side you come down on in this argument, it seems indisputable that a live annual meeting is the sole opportunity for managers and directors to greet shareholders and for shareholders to meet managers and directors. Such a golden opportunity should not be overlooked.

Virtual annual meetings may not be much different from quarterly conference calls. That begs the question, however, about the quality of today's conference calls. There is a movement among QSs and managers alike to curtail the quarterly call and cut related forecasts and guidance. The reasoning behind this movement is detailed in the chapter 7.

7

Quality Quarterly Contact

IF ANNUAL LETTERS AND MEETINGS are excellent ways to communicate to QSs, what about the rest of the year? While quarterly conference calls have been a staple of corporate life for decades, as structured today they are not congenial forums to draw many QSs or communicate useful information. When held for the purpose of providing quarterly forecasts, they can pose serious side effects. They can make CFOs resemble gold rush prospectors in Mark Twain's definition of a mine: "a mine is a hole in the ground with a liar standing over it." Therefore, many companies are considering alternatives. Let's review the debate.

Forecasts

Begin with the quarterly forecast. For one, there is no legal requirement that companies publicly predict upcoming performance. The practice of providing "quarterly guidance" began to spread in the 1980s and 1990s after decades when such forecasting was illegal.[1]

Securities laws forbade prognostications for several reasons, primarily because such predictions are given undue credence and create perverse incentives to reach them.

Once permitted, forecasting proliferated, largely in response to appetites of financial analysts. They are genuinely hungry for analytical grist such guidance provides, as it helps them make their own forecasts.

While proponents of quarterly forecasting continue to assert that more management reporting is an inexorable good, that group is becoming the minority. Most observers now recognize that the drawbacks of quarterly management forecasts far outweigh the benefits.

First, even if more information might generally be better (contestable, given today's information overload), forecasts are not information. They are predictions and guesses. Given the vicissitudes of business, no one can be highly confident in them, no matter how carefully developed.

No business operates in a predictable environment, and most face considerable volatility risk. Take examples from two very different industries showing the many risk factors that come into play. A shipping company must worry about docking and repairing vessels, moving deep-water drilling rigs, responding to hurricanes, and cleaning up oil spills; a media company must works through news cycles, election waves, sporting events, and financial gyrations.[2]

Second, it takes enormous time and effort to develop quarterly estimates, diverting managerial resources from other important business. Three-month forecasts draw attention and focus to current quarterly outcomes, away from ensuing quarters, years, or decades. As the managers at Loews Corporation quipped: "We attach a much greater priority to generating superior stock price performance over the next twelve years than over any single twelve-month period."[3]

Third, quarterly estimates become both goals and a test. Internal goal setting is necessary to measure and motivate managers.

But publicizing forecasts pushes managers to strive for those targets instead, creating perverse incentives.

Finally, a quarterly focus tempts imprudent spending cuts.[4] At Unilever, for instance, such a focus led to reducing research, technology, and investments. This form of earnings management can have disastrous effects, from distorting internal decision making to snowballing into accounting irregularities or even financial fraud.

Some recent evidence points to a decline in quarterly forecasting, with as few as one in five public companies maintaining the practice. On the other hand, many others persist, possibly out of sheer habit.[5]

Despite the conflicting evidence, one thing is clear: QSs oppose quarterly guidance. They prefer managers to focus on the long-term economics of a business, not short-run accounting results.

None of this is to say that quarterly results do not matter. They often matter a great deal, which is why law requires public companies to publish quarterly results. It's also why some companies, while skipping guidance, nevertheless still host quarterly conference calls. The key point, however, is to avoid letting quarterly events—reports, calls, or guidance—replace long-term thinking.

The balance is well stated in Markel's 2016 shareholder letter. Rather than thinking in annual terms, Markel references two other time horizons, "forever and right now." The combination stresses the urgency of business dynamics while clarifying that current decisions are not made with disappearing ink. The result for Markel is to offer quarterly calls but not forecasts—apparently the approach of an increasing number of companies today.

Most empirical research concurs. In fact, a recent study found that companies that quit forecasting came to attract a larger proportion of long-term institutional investors.[6] Quitting may be difficult over the short term, and those trying to stop face resistance and sometimes even a decline in average ensuing share price—such as Unilever, as described earlier. But the long-term advantages are strong.

Calls

Quarterly conference calls pose similar challenges to quarterly guidance. Again, neither logic nor law requires such calls. They became staples of corporate life as the forum to provide and update quarterly forecasts. Quarterly gatherings pose most of the problems that guidance does, though perhaps of smaller magnitude.

But there are potential benefits of hosting a quarterly huddle. Shareholders may have valid questions throughout the year worth addressing between annual meetings. Managers may benefit from hearing those questions and thinking them through using a shareholder perspective. In principle, it should be possible to arrange such gatherings while keeping short-term pressures in check. One step would schedule them as far away from publication of quarterly results as possible, rather than as close as possible in time, which seems to be the common pattern.

Prudence would limit discussion to past performance and strategic outlooks, rather than forecasting results. It would be a forum where executives educate shareholders to understand the business. Managers would reference recent results as briskly as possible, then focus on big-picture, long-term goals, like successful product launches, opening new markets, and gaining market share.

There are other issues with the current quarterly conference call. Despite regulatory efforts dating back two decades to assure access to all shareholders on these calls ("Regulation FD"), they remain dominated by financial analysts whose firms specialize in selling securities, with QSs in the quiet minority. While some analyst questions add value, many follow-ups do not, and while answers sometimes seem useful, many seem guarded or superficial or simply reference published materials.

Technology is also being used to erode the value of the quarterly conference call. High-frequency traders use artificial intelligence to conduct sentiment analysis while calls are in progress.

The procedure interprets the call's tone and messaging in real time and directs instant trading decisions throughout the session. The goal is to profit from a few seconds worth of "advance knowledge."

Better Ways

For managers and shareholders who hope to stay connected and engaged year-round there are a number of alternatives. The two most common alternatives are direct meetings and written questions; less common are formal shareholder liaisons and shareholder outreach programs.

Periodic Written Q&A. Companies are increasingly turning away from quarterly calls in favor of the periodic written Q&A. Companies invite shareholders to email written questions, managers prepare responses, and all are posted at times calculated to minimize any market effects. Posts are indexed and searchable on company websites.

An online Q&A can address questions from any source, not only shareholders, so long as the source is disclosed. For instance, executives might scour reliable Internet sites, such as Reddit, to address the most frequently posed questions. To be more proactive, a company could crowdsource questions from shareholders, an approach that Netflix has taken by polling shareholders online. Morningstar opted for shareholder Q&A from its beginning, and Constellation Software began the practice in 2018.

Face-to-Face Meetings. Some companies are willing to host direct meetings between shareholders and managers or even directors. Securities laws limit the scope of company disclosure to public information (under Regulation FD, if nonpublic information is disclosed to one shareholder it must be disclosed to all). But that still leaves ample room for productive talk.

Shareholders may be interested in engaging with independent directors, which can be conveniently done around the time of

the annual meeting over lunch or dinner. Take care that directors interacting with shareholders are trained to know the scope
of information that is allowable for discussion under securities
laws. If there is any doubt, they should err on the side of silence.
The boundaries should be delineated to the attending shareholders
ahead of time.

Veterans of the process suggest a few guidelines, with varying
degrees of flexibility designed to promote productive exchange
rather than straitjacket the initiative: (1) a stated policy concerning timing, topics, and shareholder participants; (2) a set of criteria
to determine which directors participate; (3) an outline of goals
or objectives for the gatherings; (4) coordination between directors and executives; and (5) legal compliance standards to avoid
impermissible disclosures.[7]

Such discussions serve to both highlight shareholder concerns
and reinforce what attracted them to the company in the first place.
Shareholders size up directors and vice versa. Conversation helps
identify areas of satisfaction as well as room for improvement.

Whether to engage should be at the discretion of directors.
Many energetically oppose the idea, while others are game.
Opponents see the outreach as investor relations, not the board's
job; supporters see it as part of corporate governance, where the
director–shareholder relationship is central. Likewise, some CEOs
will support the outreach, while others recoil at the prospect.

An example of director outreach to shareholders to educate and
align interests occurred at JPMorgan. Its directors favored maintaining the company's practice of reposing the roles of chairman
and chief executive in a single person, amid public agitation that the
two functions be separated. Directors met with shareholders, large
and small, whom they believed would listen to their reasoning.[8]
Management prevailed.

Shareholder Rewards. Companies can stay in touch with shareholders year-round—and strengthen the contact at the annual
meeting—by offering perks. Rewards tend to be gifts of company

products or price discounts. As such, they tend to attract individual shareholders, particularly those with smaller stakes, rather than institutions. Empirical research indicates that companies adopting rewards programs gain significant shifts in their shareholder lists from institutions to individuals.[9] Data as well as logic suggest that developing brand affinity entices these shareholders to stick around and support the company.[10]

Among companies boasting high QS density, a number offer such shareholder perquisites.[11] Berkshire's Geico insurance subsidiary offers shareholder discounts of 8 percent year-round. During the company's annual meeting in Omaha, all shareholders receive a 20 percent discount on all goods offered in the arena hall by scores of the company's subsidiaries, from footwear and clothing to tools and diamonds. Many local establishments join in giving the discount, including the company's Nebraska Furniture Mart and area booksellers. Its targeted product advertising entices shareholders as both consumers and investors.

In Toronto, Fairfax's numerous insurance companies offer discounts during the meeting, as do the company's local restaurants and subsidiaries selling sporting goods as well as china, silver, and giftware. For many years when Leucadia owned Crimson Wine vineyards in Napa Valley, it accompanied the pitch in its annual letters with the offer of a 20 percent discount on purchases. Crimson still offers discounts on visits and special events as well, as do other vineyards, such as Chalone Wine Group and Willamette Valley Vineyards.

Many destination offerings follow suit, with shareholder credits offered for use on cruises by both Carnival Cruise Line and Royal Caribbean and shareholders given free season passes to its dozen tracks by Churchill Downs.[12] Walt Disney's European parks continue to offer shareholder benefits, including a shareholder clubhouse, though its historical offering of passes to the Magic Kingdom in the United States seem over. Ford, IBM, and Kimberly-Clark have all offered significant product discounts to shareholders.[13]

Rewards programs can also support corporate campaigns to encourage shareholders to vote, particularly useful for persuading individual and employee shareholders. Their participation rate is far lower than that of institutions, yet among them are likely to be a sizable cohort of QSs. In particular, voting participation rates among individual shareholders is about 30 percent, compared with closer to 90 percent for institutions; support for incumbent directors and managers runs to 90 percent, while support for shareholder proposals has ranged from 36 percent to 43 percent.[14]

Although campaigns might simply emphasize how important each vote is, a more effective strategy is to offer concrete rewards for voting, without running afoul of laws that prohibit vote buying. One enticing strategy allows voting shareholders to designate charities to which the corporation allocates some of its philanthropic dollars. To minimize administrative burdens, an even easier route simply declares that the corporation will donate $1 per vote to a predetermined charity, ideally one with minimal controversy.

Bank of America increased its retail investor turnout this way two years in a row with the promise, prominently stated in its proxy statement, of donating $1 for every vote cast to the Special Olympics in 2017 and Habitat for Humanity in 2018. Individual votes increased by 8 percent the first year and 41 percent the next. These included a substantial cohort of employees, who were urged to vote through a variety of internal emails and educational videos about both the vote and the charity.

Shareholder Liaison. Finally, for those interested in a more formal and routinized approach, a shareholder liaison committee can appeal. Common among large listed French companies, these representatives regularly meet with the board of directors. On their websites, companies such as BNP Paribas and Air Liquide publish the names of the liaison committees and topics of discussion. They state that any shareholder can become a candidate for the committee, whose members typically serve three-year terms.

Board meeting agendas occasionally include time for the shareholder liaison committee. Ground rules vary: the one-way approach permits the board to ask the shareholders questions but not vice versa, whereas the two-way invites dialogue. The exchange of ideas can be productive, bringing shareholder concerns to the board's attention. While QSs regard quarterly guidance and forecasts as unnecessary, a dialogue is always valuable.

If historical performance matters more than forecasted performance, the next question is how performance should be measured. While all U.S. public companies use generally accepted accounting principles (GAAP), and most elsewhere use international financial reporting standards (IFRS), additional insight can be gained by supplemental metrics focused equally on economic value, as chapter 8 discusses.

8

Useful Metrics

LONG AGO, MANAGEMENT PROFESSOR PETER Drucker shared his view that "if you can't measure it, you can't improve it" while corporate governance professor Louis Lowenstein added that "you manage what you measure."[1] Both incontestable points raise the key issue: Which metrics should managers and investors use to measure business performance? QSs devour data and welcome managers who dive into the details with them. Demand is strong for useful long-term performance figures and analysis.

Preferred Performance Metrics

Financial reporting offers many alternative snapshot figures to portray business performance and condition. Among alternative performance metrics are economic profit, book value, and return on equity or invested capital. QSs appreciate explanations for which is preferred—and also insist on consistency in sticking with the same measure over the years, not picking and choosing depending on which looks best in any given year.

Consistency is important, because at almost any company in any given year, there is almost always a metric out there that can portray positive results. Choosing the assertions that provide silver linings is tempting—better accounts receivable turnover despite sluggish sales, faster inventory turns despite production problems, reduced debt despite greater reduction in equity.

Companies attract and keep QSs by having the courage to report the same items about the same core sources of value creation year in and year out, whether positive, negative, or neutral. QSs want the entire picture. Whatever metric is chosen, the methodology and rationale must be explained.

Economic profit is an example of a metric with great appeal for QSs. It is an honest picture of performance, taking into account multiple factors, including the cost of equity capital. CEO Brett Robert's letters to Credit Acceptance Corporation's shareholders discusses economic profit in this excerpt from his 2017 letter:

> We use a financial metric called Economic Profit to evaluate our financial results and determine incentive compensation. Economic Profit differs from GAAP net income [by subtracting] a cost for equity capital. Economic Profit is a function of three variables: the adjusted average amount of capital invested, the adjusted return on capital, and the adjusted weighted average cost of capital.

One of the pioneers of using economic profit was Roberto Goizueta, CEO of the Coca-Cola Company. He began using this measure in 1993, as reported in his ensuing 1994 letter to shareholders, presenting economic profit as a central performance metric:

> We now evaluate our business units and opportunities based primarily on their ability to generate attractive economic profit, not

just growth in revenues or earnings. We define economic profit as net operating profit after taxes, less a charge for the average cost of the capital employed to produce that profit. That shift in evaluation methodology prompted us to begin divesting ourselves of businesses with financial characteristics inferior to the remarkable fundamentals of our core soft drink business.

Companies that take economic profit seriously tend to attract QSs. Besides Coca-Cola and Credit Acceptance, these companies include Clorox, Crown Holdings, International Flavors, and Lear Corporation.[2]

Perspectives and Adjusted Metrics

It is the rare corporate executive who believes that thoroughgoing compliance with GAAP (or IFRS) produces a faithful economic statement of performance and results. That's why virtually all managers supplement their reports with adjusted and alternative metrics that, they believe, more faithfully reflect economic reality, whether economic profit or any of dozens of other refinements.

While managers must explain the accounting results, most QSs also appreciate accounting's inherent limitations. They welcome a CEO's analysis of supplemental metrics, and particularly the CEO's views of how the economics differ from the accounting.

The need for adjusted metrics and analysis may be isolated to a onetime event or may recur, spanning from a single acquisition to debate over annual amortization of intangibles. The shareholder letter is an excellent place to explain the view held by the company and its CEO, ideally in plain enough language for general understanding.

Perhaps the most recurring challenge in accounting, and its relation to economics, is the difference between accounting earnings and various formulations of economic earnings, such as

EBITDA (earnings before interest, taxes, depreciation, and amortization). While volumes are devoted to this topic, a CEO must explain the specific thinking of how these measures fit a company's particular circumstances.

Berkshire supplements its reports with a concept Buffett calls "owner earnings" for its acquired businesses, rather than relying solely on GAAP operating earnings or cash flow. Cash flows are commonly calculated as (1) GAAP operating earnings plus (2) depreciation expense and other non-cash charges.

But Buffett's owner earnings calculation subtracts one element: (3) required reinvestment in the business, or "the average amount of capitalized expenditures for plant and equipment, etc., that the business requires to fully maintain its long-term competitive position and its unit volume."

Given how common it is for (3) to exceed (2), Buffett's metric is a more useful approximation of economic reality than typical cash flow or GAAP earnings figures. Most importantly, Buffett has consistently provided this information and explained the reasoning behind it.

Warning

Despite the utility of non-GAAP measures, some managers and accountants abuse the opportunity to paint false impressions. An age-old problem, deception through non-GAAP reporting became widespread during the 1990s. Lynn Turner, then SEC chief accountant, famously quipped that using non-GAAP measures turned many financial reports into BS—Turner dubbed it "everything but the bad stuff." The pervasive problem was a factor in the accounting scandals that prompted the Sarbanes-Oxley Act of 2002, which told the SEC to regulate the practice.

In response, the SEC's Regulation G has since required companies using non-GAAP measures to reconcile them to the nearest

GAAP measure. Also banned were a variety of misleading practices that had become all too common, such as excluding various categories of expenses. Even so, non-GAAP reporting remained a fraud risk factor, prompting the SEC since 2013 to police the practice more proactively. Over the ensuing years, non-GAAP reporting has drawn a substantial volume of SEC comment letters to issuers.[3]

One clue is the invention of novel definitions of profit that myopically ignore "bad stuff." While sometimes these are specific to a particular company, the most pernicious practices become widespread across an industry or sector. For example, consider contribution margin. This purports to show selling price per unit less variable costs per unit—ignoring fixed costs. While this measure is potentially useful internally to manage a business, fixed costs cannot be ignored.

Critics pounced on such tools embraced by companies such as Peloton Interactive, Shake Shack, Uber, and WeWork's parent to exempt expenses such as rent, marketing, and stock option pay.[4] At ride-sharing companies they called it "core platform contribution profit." It reversed out expenses that, while necessary to operate the business and therefore real, did not connect to the "core platform."[5]

At WeWork's office-leasing business, for example, GAAP net income was negative. Under a notion called "community-adjusted" earnings, however, a profit was shown by ignoring a variety of necessary outlays. For one, GAAP accounting for leases requires recognizing an expense on a straight-line basis over a lease term; but some of WeWork's leases gave it rent discounts in the earlier years of the lease. Wishing to present the economics only of those early years, it opted to exclude future rent expense. That's myopic, not illuminating.

Managers interested in attracting QSs present reliable and useful financial information. They do not play games with the numbers or their investors. QSs are alert to the difference between analytical tools and legerdemain, between genuine and fake, and between the trustworthy and the charlatan.

And while discussing accounting tools and performance, it is vital to review the lumpy versus smooth debate.

Lumpy, not Smooth

Brian Bushee, who classified shareholder behavior as transient, indexed, or dedicated (quality), advises that the best way to discourage transient ownership is to avoid earnings smoothing.[6] A short-term focus demands short-term results, tempting managers to repeatedly meet short-term targets. The results are smooth reported earnings, quarter to quarter and year to year.

Managers achieving such results, however, do so by letting the accounting dog wag the economic tail, making short-term decisions around discretionary spending or otherwise to deliver ironed-out rather than wrinkly results.

Warren Buffett minted a mantra on the topic: "We won't 'smooth' quarterly or annual results: If earnings figures are lumpy when they reach headquarters, they will be lumpy when they reach you." Managers hoping to attract QSs follow suit, and rather than smoothing the lumps, they help shareholders understand the reasons behind the lumps.

If smooth accounting results reflect a short-term managerial approach prone to attracting transient shareholders, focusing on long-term economics attracts QSs. Long-term thinkers make peace with volatility, while short-term thinkers are driven to trading. As Markel's Tom Gayner elaborated in his 2013 letter:

> At many organizations, volatility causes people to go nuts. Experience has shown they are tempted to tamp it down and pretend that the world is a smooth place. We do not share this delusion. If we were irrationally afraid of volatility, we could

get rid of our equity portfolio, since equities tend to go up and down by greater percentage amounts than bonds. We think that unnaturally attempting to minimize reported volatility would diminish the long-term profitability of the company and work against the interests of long-term owners of the firm compared to short-term traders of the stock.

GAAP and IFRS offer enormous value by stating a broad set of *generally* applicable accounting principles, creating a common system that enables comparing companies across the board. But every company is unique, requiring tailored metrics to elucidate each business and its specific economics. The resulting combination of general principles coupled with specific metrics is a virtue that managers should harness. Useful and reliable accounting information is vital to directors and managers alike in discharging what QSs consider their most important function: capital allocation, discussed next.

9

Capital Allocation

"THE GOAL IS NOT TO have the longest train, but to arrive at the station first using the least fuel." This aphorism by Tom Murphy, former chairman and CEO of Capital Cities/ABC and longtime director of Berkshire Hathaway, describes the goal of successful capital allocation.

Murphy, widely considered a master of capital allocation, cautions against buying up as many companies as possible or otherwise growing for the sake of growth alone, but to get the most bang from every buck in acquisitions and other investments.

In *The Outsiders*, Will Thorndike, a student of master capital allocators, encapsulated Murphy's approach: focus on industries with attractive economic characteristics, selectively use leverage to buy occasional large properties, improve operations, pay down debt, repeat.

To drive the fastest and most efficient train, CEOs should understand capital allocation. QSs are attracted to those who do.[1]

Capital allocation is a technical term that simply denotes how corporate dollars are invested. Capital can be allocated to many different ends concurrently: fortifying the balance sheet by repaying debt or building cash reserves, funding initiatives to maintain or grow existing businesses, making acquisitions, buying back shares, or paying dividends. QSs value strong track records in capital allocation, measured by return on invested capital, and companies whose managers explain their views.

Capital allocation is, however, a practice or habit of mind learned through training and experience in investing. Although not all corporate leaders have investing backgrounds, as many rise through research, engineering, production, or sales ranks, the skill is vital and can be learned. In his 2017 letter to shareholders of Cimpress, Robert Keane stressed the link between capital allocation and success as a CEO:

> I wish that I had figured out the importance of capital allocation many years ago, but the reality is that Cimpress is just now entering our fourth year of making capital allocation an explicit focus area of our management routines so we are still learning and revising our internal processes. But better late than never: as CEO, founder and a significant shareholder, I now spend a major amount of my time on activities related to capital allocation and consider it a critical responsibility.

Phil Ordway, a quintessential QS, advocates making capital allocation an explicit corporate priority.[2] In papers and speeches, he highlights a dozen exemplary companies. These include Amazon, AutoNation, Cimpress, Credit Acceptance, Henry Schein, Morningstar, Netflix, Phillips 66, Post Holdings, Texas Instruments, and Wabco Holdings.

Framework and Measures

Figure 9.1 presents a framework for thinking about capital allocation and organizing discussion. It is not a directive or road map,

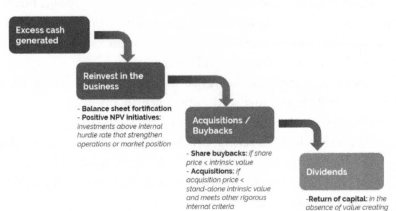

FIGURE 9.1 Capital allocation framework
Source: Author's own data.

as optimal priorities among the depicted choices will differ among companies and managers at different times. In fact, the various uses of excess cash are neither mutually exclusive nor sequential— funds can be optimally allocated to all uses and priorities given to those anywhere on the chart.

It's best to start with a general approach to measuring capital allocation effectiveness.[3] First, for any given year, calculate the corporation's average invested capital available. Begin with an estimate of the amount of money shareholders have invested. Then, each year, update by adding net income and the proceeds of any share issuances, subtracting any dividends, and adjusting for any compensation paid in shares.

Thereafter, measure overall performance as a return on the average invested capital. For example, take net income as a percentage of invested capital as an ultimate measure of capital allocation effectiveness.

To maximize return on invested capital (ROIC) on an ongoing basis, measure every corporate project accordingly. Track every allocation, including reinvestments and acquisitions, on a project-by-project basis using conventional after-tax internal rates of return (IRRs—the rate where the net present value of project cash flows are zero). Be sure all company personnel are trained to be familiar with this tool. For oversight, have the board periodically set the required hurdle rate for all project types (the minimum required IRR to green-light the proposed capital allocation).

As rigorous as this sounds, beware that IRRs are complex and future oriented and require judgment. Managers charged with related measurement may naturally tend to overestimate. To compensate for this, compute an additional measure of overall annual capital allocation effectiveness. Consider one that is simpler, historical, and less judgment laden: add annual ROIC to annual growth in organic revenue (not acquired) and compare the sum to the hurdle rate.

The tools can be adapted to all of the capital allocation opportunities presented in figure 9.1. Such an approach is an excellent way to attract QSs.

Management at Texas Instruments has done so. It sees capital allocation as a top priority. The company has long been a conscious and successful cultivator of QSs. In fact, among its original investors, in a private placement, was Phil Fisher. That quintessential QS never sold the stock, adding to his position over the years to make it one of his largest.

Today, while Texas Instruments faces the usual ownership by the major indexers (together owning some 20 percent), an impressive QS cohort accompanies them: Prime Capital Management, Massachusetts Financial Services, T. Rowe Price, Capital Research Global Investors, Capital World Investors, Henderson Group, Capital International Investors, Franklin, AllianceBernstein, State Farm, Bessemer Group, and Davis Selected Advisers. A concise statement of capital allocation is easily accessible on the investor's section of the Texas Instruments website, excerpted below. Such transparency and accountability are compelling to QSs.

Texas Instruments: Capital Allocation Principles

Our capital management strategy reflects our belief that free cash flow growth, especially on a per-share basis, is most important to maximizing value over the long term, and that free cash flow will be valued only if it is productively reinvested in the business or returned to owners. Our business model and competitive advantages have enabled our company consistently to generate solid free cash flow margins. Our free cash flow per share has been steady and growing over the past 10 years despite, at times, difficult macroeconomic or market environments.

Our strong balance sheet enables us to fully fund pensions and have access to low-cost debt. With interest rates still low, we plan to continue to hold debt as long as it makes economic sense. Even then, we use debt judiciously such that we avoid concentrated maturities while we maintain our strategic flexibility. Combined, these elements allow us to invest for our future and still have excess cash available to return to owners. Over a 10-year period, 2009–2018, we allocated $77 billion across these areas:

- $32 billion on R&D, sales and marketing, capital expenditures, and cash used for inventory to support the organic growth of our businesses. Our R&D expenditures are disciplined and focused on markets we believe have the greatest growth potential. . . .
- $25 billion on consistent share repurchases, intended to generate the accretive capture of free cash flow for long-term investors. We focus on consistent repurchases when the stock price is below the intrinsic value, using reasonable growth assumptions.
- $13 billion on dividends, designed to appeal to our broader set of investors, with a focus on sustainability and dividend growth.
- $7 billion on acquisitions to fund inorganic growth. . . . We look at an acquisition opportunity through two lenses. First, it must be a strategic match, which for us translates into an entity that is analog- and catalog-focused with a high exposure to industrial and automotive. Second, it must meet certain financial

> performance levels such that it generates a return on invested capital greater than our weighted average cost of capital, as one example, in about four years. . . .
>
> Our goal is to return all of our free cash flow to owners in the form of dividends and stock repurchases. We have a robust model to allocate returns between dividend growth and stock repurchases.

Let's turn to some particulars.

Reinvestment

While there is fluidity to capital allocation, the first priority ought to belong to reinvestment in current businesses to increase competitive advantage. The chief concerns for corporate leadership and QSs are managerial rationalizations about the prospects of such a use of capital. Managers are often optimistic, usually a desirable trait in an entrepreneur, but not in excess. Standard measurements, such as IRR and hurdle rates, along with related oversight, help keep them in check.

Another aspect of reinvestment is fortifying the balance sheet. Companies need sufficient liquidity to be prepared for economic distress as well as to take advantage of fruitful opportunities. As the Tisch family executives at Loews Corporation point out, it's easier to raise money when you can than when you need to.[4] Striking the happy medium is key, however, as hoarding too much cash on the balance sheet could be embarrassing to directors and officers alike.

Leadership at Sherwin-Williams adopts and explains a clear and consistent capital allocation philosophy. It takes a somewhat

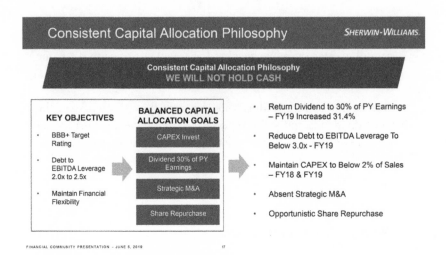

FIGURE 9.2 Consistent capital allocation philosophy
Source: Sherwin-Williams, "Financial Overview," Financial Community Presentation, June 5, 2019, https://investors.sherwin-williams.com/doc/fcp _financial_overview_2019.

extreme position in its aversion to holding cash, preferring other uses or distributions to shareholders (figure 9.2, a slide from a 2019 Sherwin-Williams' CEO presentation, emphasizes this point).

Not all companies will find this approach congenial, as many prefer to strengthen the balance sheet or preserve capital for opportunities down the road.

The takeaway: it works for Sherwin-Williams; the company has explained its framework and how that framework suits its business, culture, and goals. And there is a track record, including an enviable roster of QSs at the top of the shareholder list: Capital World Investors, Massachusetts Financial Services, FMR, Fiera Capital, Henderson Group, AllianceBernstein, T. Rowe Price, Meritage Group, Findlay Park, Capital Research Global Investors, Farallon Capital Management, and Chilton Investment Company.

Acquisitions

Next up are acquisitions of new businesses. The capital allocation test is simple: whether the acquisition makes current shareholders wealthier on a per-share basis. That means paying a price less than the target company's stand-alone value, ideally delivering an expected return (IRR) that exceeds a preset hurdle rate.

Despite the simple test, acquisitions are a common source of capital destruction. What's essential in this step is skepticism of optimistic scenarios, such as forecasts of value arising from synergies or other opportunities expected to materialize postacquisition.

Improving an acquired company's operations postacquisition is a source of value creation. But managers do not always provide investors with sufficient information to evaluate proposed acquisitions completely or objectively. They provide projections that look compelling and business rationales that seem logical.

Yet acquisitions can be emotional, exciting managers and stoking optimism. Managers cultivate QSs by playing down expectations from acquisitions, skipping talk of synergies and other often-elusive veins of value. An even better approach: conducting ongoing, constantly updated postacquisition analysis to compare expected IRR with actual ROIC and determining reasons for the difference.

Another source of discipline is using cash in preference to stock to pay for acquisitions. Using stock can inflate the price, often felt as play money, more like poker chips than cash.

Henry Schein, a dental and health-care products and distribution business, has had some fantastic results in using a value-based approach in capital allocation, including when evaluating acquisitions. It has made more than two hundred acquisitions in recent decades and invested heavily in organic growth, new product lines, and new geographies. A baker's dozen from 2015 to 2019 were presented as "key," noted in figure 9.3.

Dental Market – Key Acquisitions

Key Acquisitions	Description	LTM Revenue*
Cliniclands (2019)	Entry into dental market in Sweden	$10M
Wuhan (2019)	Expands our dental business in China	$40M
Medentis/Intra-Lock/Pro-Cam (2018)	Strengthens Global Dental Implant Offerings	$45M
Ortho2 (2017)**	Advances orthodontic software offering	$14M
Edge Endo (2017)	Expands our line of Endodontic Solutions	$17M
SAS (2017)	Enhances Dental Surgical Supply offering	$72M
Marrodent (2016)	Entry into Poland Dental Market	$32M
CAP (2016)	Expands Lab Supply Business in the U.S.	$30M
One Piece (2016)**	Expands our Dental Business in Japan	$125M
Dental Cremer (2016)	Expands our Dental Business in Brazil	$145M
Dental Trey (2015)	Builds on our Dental Business in Italy	$49M

* Last 12 months revenue at time of acquisition in USD
** Not consolidated

HENRY SCHEIN 13

FIGURE 9.3 Dental market—key acquisitions
Source: Henry Schein, "Q3 2019" investors' presentation, https://www.henryschein.com/us-en/images/Corporate/IRPresentation.pdf.

Share Buybacks

At least one capital allocation decision can directly improve the quality of the shareholder base: share buybacks. When companies buy their own shares, the most likely cohort interested in meeting the demand are transients, who by definition are prepared to sell at all times. That automatically increases the proportion of shares held by longer-term shareholders, such as QSs.

But share buybacks are only rational for shareholders if the company pays a price less than a conservative estimate of the company's per-share intrinsic value. If so, that is prudent capital allocation; if not, it is capital squandering.

Buybacks were uncommon through the 1970s and 1980s, as dividends were the popular route for corporate distributions to shareholders.[5] Pioneers stood out, including Roberto Goizueta at Coca-Cola, Larry Tisch at Loews Corporation, Henry Singleton at Teledyne, and Kay Graham at the Washington Post Co. In that era, these companies followed the textbook, repurchasing shares as a capital allocation exercise, when no better alternatives existed and price was below value.[6]

By the late 1990s, buybacks had become a common practice across corporate America. Such proliferation raised a new concern: whether managers possessing superior valuation information exploit selling shareholders when buying at a discount. To address this, managers must provide shareholders with all relevant valuation information. Otherwise, insiders take advantage of uninformed shareholders, confiscating their interests at pennies on the dollar—anathema to QSs.

The advice Warren Buffett gives to investors applies equally to managers making capital allocation decisions: be fearful when others are greedy, and greedy when others are fearful. The most obvious application of this investment principle in the context of capital allocation concerns share buybacks. Companies make errors of both commission—buying no matter how high the price—and omission—failing to buy when prices plummet.

Two exemplary exceptions to the latter problem win honors in this area. One is Sherwin-Williams, the paint manufacturer, whose policy of holding no cash and buying shares back cheaply paid off during the financial crisis of 2008–2009. Financial markets swooned, despair was in the air, and many companies put the brakes on their share buybacks. Not Sherwin-Williams, whose persistent buying through the crisis generated considerable shareholder value for continuing owners—a practice QSs applaud and one that is almost certainly attributable to having in place a clear and consistent capital allocation policy.[7]

Another honorable mention for opportunistic share buybacks in adherence with a capital allocation framework goes to Wabco, an international trucking technology company. In late 2011, the Euro crisis loomed, casting a pall over much of the continent, especially in Greece. Talk of a double-dip recession punished equity prices across the market, falling particularly heavily on Wabco. The company went bullish, increasing repurchases substantially. When reporting on the enhanced program, the company also stressed confidence, assuaged fears, and clarified some misconceptions.

Buybacks automatically increase earnings per share (EPS) and tend to boost stock prices. QSs are alert to these effects and oppose managers whose buybacks are motivated by such results rather than by rational capital allocation. They are therefore skeptical of buyback formulas or quotas. Moreover, since buybacks automatically boost EPS, if that metric is an important part of managerial performance reviews or compensation, boards must be especially vigilant to deter share buybacks designed to boost executive pay.

Finally, when choosing between paying a cash dividend or buying back shares, the effects on shareholders and option holders differ greatly. Dividends increase returns to shareholders but decrease the value of options, while buybacks boost earnings per share and therefore increase option value. A conflict of interest looms between what is best for managers holding options and all other shareholders. That's why QSs are skeptical of companies with significant executive stock option compensation coupled with significant share buybacks. In many such cases, a better capital allocation for shareholders would be dividends.

Dividends

Dividends are another capital allocation decision that can directly shape the shareholder base. Regular dividends give shareholders a reason to stick around during troubled patches—they can be a useful magnet that lengthens holding periods and sometimes induces taking larger positions. This point was stressed by one of the more frenetic and diversified stock pickers, Peter Lynch, who gained fame as both a stock picker and author.[8]

A small group of companies boast of paying an increasing dividend over the past five decades. A few examples, all of which are high on the list of attracting QSs: Coca-Cola, Dover, Genuine Parts, Hormel Foods, Johnson & Johnson, and Procter & Gamble. Even sustaining regular dividend increases for one decade is difficult, with fewer than three hundred companies having managed to do so of late.

At the other end of the spectrum are companies that have not paid dividends, either ever or in recent memory. The reasons are mixed, running the gamut from dazzling growth opportunities to trouble meeting bills. Whatever the direction taken, it is best for CEOs always to explain capital allocation policy and choices in their annual shareholder letters.

Board Oversight

Corporate law requires that boards approve major acquisitions and dividends and, as a practical matter, share buyback programs.[9] Along with such approvals, good practice dictates that the board's principal role is setting applicable hurdle rates for reinvestment and acquisitions.

Companies wishing to make capital allocation a priority could revisit whether to create a board committee with this oversight. At S&P 500 companies, boards maintain an average of four committees, and about one-third include a committee on capital allocation, finance, or investment.[10] Among the few with such committees are AutoNation, Regency Centers, and Playa Hotels. Charters might call for postinvestment reviews on all important allocations, especially organic growth initiatives, acquisitions, and share buybacks.

If one advantage of cultivating QSs is developing relationships and potential directors, capital allocation is an area where QSs can add particularly rich value. The experience at Credit Acceptance attests to this. The company's capital allocation is clear and consistent, stressing fundamentals of hurdle rates across the board and the difference between price and value when repurchasing stock. Virtually every Credit Acceptance annual shareholder letter for many years has included some version of the following assertion: "We have used our excess capital to repurchase shares only when prices are at or below our estimate of intrinsic value."

The CEO of Credit Acceptance, a leading operator in the industry, has acknowledged that two of his directors recruited from the QS community are better than he at capital allocation. So long as a board boasts some such expertise, and the rest of the board learns from them, there's no need for a capital allocation committee.

The board must implement capital allocation principles across all decisions, which may sometimes lead a company to a variety of strategic transactions such as sales, spins, splits, or trackers—topics up next.

10

Trackers and Spins

CONVENTIONAL WISDOM SAYS THAT "The whole is greater than the sum of its parts." But often the opposite is true, and the parts are more valuable on their own.

For companies, a simple way to capture that greater value would be to sell the higher-value parts. While commonplace, doing so poses adverse tax consequences that destroy rather than enhance shareholder value. Many better alternative approaches have been devised to solve this problem, channeling value to shareholders, while offering the added advantages of segmenting the shareholder base and attracting QSs.

Collectively called "separation" transactions, these are well-known, if exotic, structures such as tracking stocks, public offerings of minority interests in subsidiaries, and spin-offs. Separation trans-actions produce potential benefits for both the parent and the newly independent business. The parent may gain from a sharper focus on its core retained businesses—along with improved pricing rational-ity of its stock—and the separated business may gain from its new status as an autonomous entity freshly nurtured by that parent.

From the viewpoint of shaping the shareholder base, these trans-actions offer additional benefits: tracking stocks can create inter-nal business delineations to separate QSs from transients, with QSs tied to a core business and transients to the non-core business. Spin-offs of non-core businesses can be designed to appease, deter, or thwart activists. These and similar transactions sometimes trig-ger screens that result in companies being excluded from major indexes such as the S&P 500—a benefit to any company wishing to reduce the density of indexers in its shareholder base.

Trackers

The simplest and most obvious way to segment the shareholder base is to create multiple tracking stocks for a single company.[1] This technique is designed to match different shareholder bases to different businesses, without legally separating them. For exam-ple, a business requiring long-term R&D investment with long product cycles should attract longer-term shareholders, while one selling quotidian commodities at spot prices might attract shorter-term shareholders.

Tracking stocks, corporate equity of a parent tied to the eco-nomic performance of a subsidiary, were the 1984 brainchild of Georgetown University tax professor Martin D. Ginsburg, late husband of Justice Ruth Bader Ginsburg. Professor Ginsburg's design, still used to this day, solved a problem for H. Ross Perot, the colorful Texas billionaire.

In 1984, when General Motors acquired Mr. Perot's company, Electronic Data Systems, he and his many employee-shareholders were concerned that EDS's performance would be lost within the GM behemoth. They wanted to ensure that superior performance of EDS would be rewarded regardless of how the rest of GM performed, due to the relative time horizons of each company. The solution: the EDS group accepted shares in GM, but performance was tied to the economics and related time horizons of EDS, aptly dubbed "Class E stock."

Professor Ginsburg's invention was so effective that GM copied it the next year when acquiring Hughes Aircraft Company—using currency dubbed GM "Class H stock." Both trackers remained in place for more than a decade until GM spun the companies off, distributing all GM's stock in them to GM shareholders to form freestanding companies. GM's tracking stock worked well for all concerned, especially Mr. Perot, who showed his gratitude by endowing a professorship at Georgetown: the Martin D. Ginsburg Chair in Taxation.

The Ginsburg Model. When corporations issue stock, stockholders enjoy many rights against that issuer; boards control the whole and owe associated duties to all stockholders; and governments levy associated taxes. Trackers splice rights to different shareholder groups, without relinquishing board prerogatives or repudiating duties, while simultaneously deferring tax consequences.

The terms of tracking stock put parental control in its board, provide mechanisms to track the economic performance of the targeted business, and set policies for dealings between parental units to be at arm's length. Boards often adopt dividend policies based on cash flows of targeted businesses, retain power to convert tracking stock into the parent's common stock (an "unwind" feature), and pledge to redeem the stock upon the sale of the tracked business's assets. Otherwise, tracking stock terms are the same as the parent's ordinary common stock for matters such as voting rights and rights upon parent liquidation, although some variation is possible.

Exact advantages of tracking stock structures vary depending on the specific features of the various businesses and how they interact. Benefits may include offsetting tax benefits when one business generates substantial taxable profits while another incurs substantial losses; combined balance sheet strength equating to lower borrowing costs; immunization from antitrust laws that might prohibit two independent businesses from coordination that is perfectly legal among business units of the same family; and adding incentives for managers to enhance the performance of businesses they run by compensating them with their own tracking stock.

Trackers' Rise. The original tracker model, tailor-made for GM's acquisitions, was soon adapted to other settings. In 1991–1992, U.S. Steel Corporation enjoyed synergies through common control of such diverse subsidiaries as Delhi Group and Marathon Oil, which shared gas-processing plants and enjoyed lower borrowing costs together than if independent. But the businesses had distinct economics, so a tracking stock would both keep the advantages of common control while increasing visibility into the tracked business, with gains for stockholders and managers alike. The solution worked for a decade until USX spun Marathon Oil off.

In 1995, after the government's antitrust breakup of AT&T, US West was a regional telephone company that also owned cable and cellular assets. Long-term investors attracted to the stability of the telephone utility might recoil at the volatility of media assets; shorter-term investors seeking rapid growth would have opposite tastes. Trackers satisfied the demand of each while housing all operations under common control, harvesting related synergies. To further meet investor tastes, the utility side would pay regular dividends as the media side would reinvest earnings. And the arrangement could be unwound as circumstances changed: in fact, in 1998, after synergies proved elusive, US West spun off the media business.

In the mid-1990s, the iconic investor and telecom mogul, John Malone, used trackers to segment the economics of diverse media assets he had been acquiring for decades through Tele-Communications Inc. (TCI). In addition to other advantages ranging from antitrust to tax, Malone realized that cable assets along with programming, for example, were better combined than separate from an operations perspective. Yet they featured different economic attributes. Using tracking stocks for such businesses could translate into higher price–earnings multiples, which can be valuable when using stock to acquire other companies.

The TCI transactions were distinct in both complexity and boldness, which drew critics. They referenced conflicts of interest between siblings that all parent boards using trackers face. TCI's prospectus said as much, then simply avowed confidence in its directors' ability to discharge their duties. This amounted to an "implicit message of 'trust us,' " critics said, urging such boards to establish structural cures, such as independent committees. But no governance devices can resolve such problems, and one truth about trackers is that, to make them beneficial for all parties, the parent's board must be trustworthy.

Stumble and Fall. As QS Bill Ruane once lamented: on Wall Street, the process goes from innovation to imitation to irrationality. The same held for trackers, as they proliferated in the late 1990s technology sector amid irrational exuberance fueling the bubble. A common theme featured a traditional company offering trackers in an Internet subsidiary: bookseller Barnes & Noble for its e-tailing operations; the Walt Disney Company with Go.com; brokerage firm Donaldson, Lufkin & Jenrette for its online trading business, DLJdirect; and publisher Ziff Davis for its online operations, ZD.net.

Nearing a peak, in mid-2000 about thirty listed trackers traded—half issued during the bubble—and several then pending were soon aborted, including tracking stocks for DuPont's life sciences business, the *New York Times* online, and Staples .com. Others soon wound down, including at Disney and DLJ (then owned by Credit Suisse). While the market for tech recovered, appetite for trackers remained dim. Although a few trackers launched in 2001 and 2002, none debuted during 2003 or 2004.

Skeptics included luminaries from the value investing world such as Columbia Business School professor Bruce Greenwald and *Wall Street Journal* veteran Roger Lowenstein. They challenged many companies' trackers as "putting lipstick on a pig" or "rearranging deck chairs on the Titanic." Proponents of efficient market theory could not imagine how ownership structures could affect the market's valuation of businesses.

During the bubble, many companies used trackers less to solve a knotty business problem—which could as easily be resolved by separately audited financials—than to follow frothy markets. Many issuers lacked the compelling rationale that makes trackers suitable—operational synergies, interdependence, tax efficiency, or acquisition opportunities. It was not enough to repeat versions of the US West story—which had in any event faltered.

But despite the broad retreat from trackers, Malone saw them as an ideal solution for numerous challenges he faced managing Liberty Media. By 2005, Liberty was a complex group of diverse media assets needing simplification. Malone began by spinning off two businesses—a collection of international media assets and a 50 percent stake in Discovery Communications. Still, Liberty Media perceived continued stock market undervaluation—by as much as 70 percent.

To address these challenges, Liberty Media created trackers, Liberty Interactive (LINTA) and Liberty Capital (LCAPA). LINTA was anchored by Liberty's 98 percent interest in QVC, the television shopping channel and a strong cash generator, and included the company's 22 percent interest in Expedia, the online travel agency, and a 22 percent stake in InterActivCorp (IAC), owner of such companies as Ask Jeeves and Ticketmaster.

LCAPA would house all other assets, including, as the prospectus explained, "video programming and communications technology and services involving cable, satellite, the Internet and other distribution media as they evolve"—in other words, anything telecom related. These assets included a variety of businesses and securities, such as the wholly owned Starz, public equity in Motorola and News Corp., and a variety of complex hedging instruments.

Liberty thus created two sets of assets of appeal to different types of investors. Those who favored predictable cash flows from QVC and other straightforward stalwarts would be more attracted to LINTA; those wanting to bet on Malone's record of buying and selling a variety of diverse media assets and financial hedging transactions could gravitate toward LCAPA.

When trackers increase a company's aggregate valuation, that strengthens a company's hand in acquisitions it pays for using stock. For Liberty Media, this proved valuable by 2008 in the depths of the financial crisis, when LCAPA acquired satellite radio operator SiriusXM. With a total return exceeding thirty-eight times its initial investment (to date), this is among the most successful investments of the century, outdoing even those famously executed during the crisis by Warren Buffett.

Critics would say that if parent stock is undervalued, a board can intensify buyback programs until the stock corrects, and if a company is too complex, it should be simplified. On the other hand, Liberty had tried both buybacks and spin-offs, but undervaluation persisted. Costs of the tracking structure include internal managerial resources to design and implement it, along with external costs of educating analysts and investors on the rationales. But these costs are not great and, if the program fails, it can readily be unwound, also at modest incremental cost.

The issue came down to a venerable debate, whether trackers are mere financial engineering—in the purely negative sense of doing nothing to increase underlying fundamental value—or a financial achievement that increases value by deftly combining assets to cater to different investor appetites while maintaining economic efficiency. Given the dot-com experience, the verdict for almost all companies was in, but for Malone and Liberty Media, the jury was still out.

After all, the same critical logic would denounce spin-offs, yet history proves their value—and, for that matter, the dot-com era aside, history had proven the value of trackers. Today, history appears to be on the side of trackers: in 2008, the *Wall Street Journal* declared them "relics" on the "verge of extinction."

In 2016, tax lawyers from Fried Frank—where Professor Ginsburg once worked—proclaimed, with apologies to Mark Twain, that reports of the death of trackers are "greatly exaggerated." A new wave of trackers had emerged, offering compelling rationales.

Revival. In 2013, Fantex, whose business consists of separate branding contracts with professional athletes, offered trackers tied to the economic value of those contracts; in 2014, Fidelity National Financial Inc., a title insurance company with an investment strategy focused on individual businesses, offered trackers tied to its core business as well as those investees; in 2016, Dell used tracking stock as part of its purchase of EMC Corp., tracking EMC's 80 percent–owned subsidiary, VMWare Inc., a publicly traded software company.

Researchers at Merrill Lynch published a paper in 2016 identifying all the familiar benefits as well as costs and stressed that trackers are only advisable when a company can offer a compelling rationale. It devoted a full page to depicting nearly a dozen Liberty Media trackers and said: "The tracking stocks and spin-offs issued by Liberty from 2004–2015 have resulted in an out-performance vs. the S&P 500 Index of >200 percent for the Liberty investor."

Aside from segmenting the shareholder base between transients and QSs, trackers may also dramatically reduce the indexing cohort. This is because many index providers, such as the S&P 500, exclude companies with tracking stocks from their index—as some likewise do for companies with dual-class capital structures.

Spins

In recent years, amid calls for focusing rather than diversifying, managers find it increasingly difficult to justify conglomerates. A few companies have justified sprawling diversity on organizational grounds—Berkshire is a prominent example, but widely seen as one-of-a-kind, too exceptional to be used as a model for public companies, at least outside the insurance industry. For most, attempts at justification fall flat and invite activists, who push for prompt divestitures. To avoid that fate, and win over QSs, a regular program of growth and trimming may make more sense.

Activists have long favored spin-offs, the most common form of separation transaction. A parent corporation declares a tax-free dividend to all its shareholders of stock in a subsidiary business to be separated. Upon payment of the dividend, the spun business becomes a freestanding independent entity.

Spin-offs were a familiar type of corporate transaction in the 1990s, with some 325 closed that decade.[2] Thereafter, interest slowed to a fraction of that through 2015, but from there interest renewed, and they have become more frequent. Prominent spins—all instigated by activist investors—include eBay spinning PayPal (at the urging of Carl Icahn); EMC spinning VMWare (Elliott Management); and Timken spinning its steel business (Relational Investors).

Consider Danaher Corporation, a conglomerate operating in several industries and across multiple platforms, founded in 1983 by brothers Mitchell and Steven Rales, who still own 12 percent of the stock, although they long ago ceded their managerial roles. In 2015, activist Third Point signaled a taste for breakup, acquiring a small stake that ultimately represented less than half of 1 percent of the stock.[3] At the time, Danaher boasted at least thirty long-term shareholders allocating more than 3 percent of their portfolios to the company, a group aggregating several times the activist's stake, as well as several others with slightly smaller portfolio positions yielding meaningful percentages of the outstanding shares.[4]

With such supportive long-term shareholders reinforcing the Rales' ownership, Danaher successfully navigated the activist pressure, without necessarily defeating Third Point. It took a two-step process that allowed it to continue as it always has. First, it closed on its largest acquisition ever; second, it combined that company with some related assets—in industrial tools—into a new company that it then spun off as a stand-alone with $6 billion in revenue. Danaher retained the rest of its business—less sprawling, but a diverse group of life science companies with $17 billion in revenue, still run the Danaher way, meaning an acquisitive, diversified, decentralized industrial corporation.

Across decades, spins have had multiple uses. They have been used to separate businesses lacking a continuing strategic fit, such as when AT&T spun off Lucent and NCR in 1996. They have been used to break up conglomerates, such as when ITT split into three in 1995. In 1998, Alleghany Corporation, under the leadership of renowned investor-manager John Burns, spun off its Chicago Title Corporation business, creating a major new independent insurance company with an initial market capitalization exceeding $1 billion.

Some managers have used spins to clean up a business plagued by problems, as occurred with numerous spins out of Tyco International in the years following its financial scandals. A wave of spin-offs involved separating an operating company's real estate interests—often into tax-advantaged real estate investment trusts—at such companies as Macy's and MGM Resorts.

The results can be mixed, however. A notable serial spinner is IDT Corporation, founded and long run by Howard Jonas, succeeded in 2014 by his son. The company and its founder are highly regarded and have achieved substantial shareholder returns, though unevenly. Effecting spins has been a part of the standard practice—some have performed exceptionally well, others the opposite.

To illustrate, Straight Path Communications, a 2013 spin that began trading around $5 per share, rose by 2019 to $180, but Zedge, a 2016 spin that began trading at just above $7, was in 2019 trading below $2. In between, the stock of IDW Media, a 2009 spin, began around $2 and rose to as high as around $40, before retreating in 2019 to $17. Spins are not for the faint of heart, but QSs will be attracted to learn more from managers willing to engage with the idea.

John Malone is also an avid proponent of spin-offs, matching his enthusiasm for tracking stocks. Liberty Media is constantly making acquisitions, but also constantly divesting, whether directly in selling interests or, more often, in slicing them through spin-offs (or trackers). Prominent spin-offs include Liberty Global/ Discovery, DirecTV, Liberty Global, Starz, and QVC.

The spin-off pushes interests back and outside the entity, negating conglomerate; rather than creating an empire under consolidated rule, it is as if the king hives off earldoms, dukedoms, and other fiefdoms and locates them where their value will be best appreciated.

Underlying the trackers and spins, as well as the rest of Malone's approach, are optimizing leverage, efficient taxation, and opportunistic deal making. In addition, such structures lead to internal growth of talented managers and better incentive programs. The output from these efforts are extraordinary shareholder returns, a compound annual growth rate since 2006 of roughly 18 percent.

Uniting the most successful spins is how the value of both the parent and the spun company improves. This often arises when the spin-off's value is suppressed within the larger parent. The dynamics are explained well by another early and frequent engineer of spin-offs, William Stiritz, longtime CEO of Ralston Purina:[5]

> The problem with large corporations, where they've developed a centralized command structure over multiple divisions is that they are less creative, less adaptive, less inventive than a company that is spun out and freestanding. Spinouts are better-incented and their managers will think about the task much more intentionally. They are the ultimate form of reorganization for better results.

Ralston Purina, the sprawling food products company, had grown to include a variety of businesses, collectively called Ralcorp, in many unrelated niche areas—infant formula, cereal such as Raisin

Bran, cookies, and ski resorts! The businesses did not fit the core
and suffered benign neglect. Stiritz explains:

> Ralcorp is a case study of a group of assets that originally were
> buried within the corporate conglomerate. It was three or four
> layers down in terms of management levels, an insignificant
> hobby business, with low returns. What do you do with it? [He
> spun it out as] a way to create a new organizational model.
> I stayed with Ralcorp as its chairman, inserted its management,
> and allocated the resources of the company to what we should
> be doing.

After spinning off certain businesses, Stiritz observed a trans-
formation in corporate leadership. Many Ralcorp managers
who showed modest abilities beforehand became "incredible
managers." Stiritz attributed the result to a newfound managerial
zeal in the separate businesses.

Spins have become increasingly common in recent years as a
way to increase focus and related capital allocation, whether at
conglomerates or otherwise. As such, a strategy that includes
spin-offs as a regular element can be a strong general deterrent to
activists, as well as a source of shareholder value.

Spins, trackers, and public subsidiary initial public offerings
are often value-enhancing structures in the divvying up of corporate equity. By channeling value to shareholders, they both
increase the total value available while also helping to segment
the shareholder base. In these ways, managers and directors not
only offer the menu with the greatest value, but cater within the
menu to the many different shareholder appetites out there.

PART III
Pivot Points

THIS PART HIGHLIGHTS THREE SALIENT features of corporate governance: director selection, executive pay, and shareholder voting. These are three of the most important topics in corporate life. But they have been chosen principally because of how their unusual history has led to a point where different shareholders have quite different approaches to the subjects.

On director selection, while historically done by incumbent executives and directors, shareholders have gained greater sway. Yet approaches differ: indexers adopt general templates denominating "good directors," activists nominate particular individuals to advance their proffered business plans, and QSs focus on firm-specific criteria.

Executive pay, long a hot-button issue, has only recently become a shareholder focal point, since laws requiring shareholder votes passed after the 2008 financial crisis. While activists rarely campaign on the subject and indexers rarely vote *no* on pay, QSs are more likely to dive into the numbers to form an independent view.

While ultimate responsibility for executive pay remains with boards, they benefit from the more studious approach.

On shareholder voting, while historically one share–one vote, alternative voting regimes have been emerging, due to both the fragmentation of the shareholder population and the growing number of topics put to shareholder votes—from director elections to say on pay and beyond.

Dual-class structures proliferate in response to incumbent aversion to activist risk. *Time-weighted* voting—shares get more votes the longer they are held—gains attention as a way to deter transients yet augments the power of long-term indexers. This book introduces a variation: quality voting to attract QSs—shares get more votes in the hands of long-term concentrated shareholders.

11

Director Selection
Stewards, Advocates, or Walkovers?

THE BOARD WON THE HIGHEST marks for outstanding corporate governance. It boasted fifteen distinguished members independent of management, had numerous committees all composed solely of independent directors, who were diverse in terms of race, gender, and skill sets—all as displayed in a matrix on the company's website—and the roles of chairperson and CEO were held by different people.

A noted scorer of governance "best practices" voted it one of the best five boards in corporate America. Under this board's oversight, the company it led collapsed in a multi-billion-dollar flameout. The company was Enron. In the two decades since its implosion, corporate players have debated the board's role and director selection and boards continue to struggle in their oversight, as attested to by challenges besetting major companies from Boeing to Wells Fargo.

People generally agree that board oversight is as or more important than ever. But they disagree on how to make the selection. Some stress focusing on substance—director personality and philosophy—while others stress process—board features such as independence, committees, matrixes depicting diversity, and splitting the roles of CEO and chairperson.

Today's shareholder cohorts take different approaches to the director-selection process. Through the 1970s, corporate directors were chosen by chief executives, who valued shared outlooks and offered unwavering support. From the 1980s through the early 2000s, institutional shareholders gained a greater voice in the selection process as they applied pressure to appoint directors with greater independence. Today, that voice is as fragmented as the shareholder base it is supposed to serve.

While it is difficult to determine, empirically, which methods or structures are superior, it is illuminating to highlight some of the important differences among the approach to director selection by today's dominant shareholder cohorts.

Seeking Stewards

QSs seek directors with a shareholder orientation, business savvy, and interest in the particular company and its stewardship. They are more interested in those particular director traits, and the specific context of a given company, than in following general formulas or perceived best practices.[1]

The number one question QSs have about any director candidates, however, is whether they are shareholder oriented. That is, all directors should act as if there is a single absentee owner and do everything reasonably possible to advance that owner's long-term interest.

This is not a mandate for the immediate maximization of shareholder value, but rather a mentality to evaluate every decision from the shareholder perspective. To that end, it is desirable for directors to buy and hold sizable personal stakes in companies they serve, so that they truly walk in the shoes of owners.

The board's most important job is selecting an outstanding CEO. If the board secures an outstanding CEO, it will likely face few other major problems. All CEOs must be measured according to a set of performance standards. A board's outside directors must formulate these standards and regularly evaluate the CEO in light of them—without the CEO being present.

Standards should be tailored to the particular business culture but should stress fundamental baselines, such as returns on shareholder capital and progress in market value per share over multiple years. Above all, directors should evaluate the CEO's record on capital allocation measured against a hurdle rate the board sets.

Directors need to think independently to tighten the wiggle room that "long-term" gives to CEOs: although corporate leaders should think in terms of years, not quarters, they must not rationalize sustained subpar performance by perpetual pleas to shareholder patience. After all, long-term can be excessive, passing into a euphemism for endless mediocrity. The solution: directors who insist on achieving measurable intermediate goals as well.

If the CEO's performance persistently falls short of the standards set by the directors, then the board must replace the CEO. The same goes for all other senior managers boards oversee, just as an intelligent owner would if present. In addition, the directors must be the stewards of owner capital to contain any managerial overreach that dips into shareholders' pockets. Such pickpocketing can range from imperious acquisition sprees to managerial enrichment through interested transactions or even myopia amid internal scandal and related crisis.

In addressing these problems, the director's actions must be fair, swift, and decisive. Directors who perceive a managerial problem should immediately alert other directors to the issue. If enough are persuaded, concerted action can be readily coordinated to resolve the problem.

Here, too, shareholders can play a role. As discussed in chapter 7, companies can make their directors available to their largest long-term QSs. These representatives can discuss issues put to shareholder votes that affect enduring value. A few influential QSs, acting together, can effectively reform a given company's corporate governance simply by withholding their votes for directors who are tolerating odious behavior.

Activist Nominees

Activist shareholders regularly identify and recruit able director nominees to serve on boards of corporations they target. These director nominees are often experts in the relevant industry or on aspects of perceived board weaknesses, such as corporate governance. They may often be the kinds of directors QSs would seek and nominate themselves. But the context wherein such nominations arise can compromise actual or perceived stewardship.

First, there is long-standing concern that directors appointed as the result of activist support will be more beholden to the activist than to the other shareholders. This concern is constrained somewhat by a director's fiduciary duties, which require acting for the corporation, not any particular shareholder.

But circumstances can aggravate the problem. For instance, some activists have offered their nominees bonuses for achieving stated corporate results during their tenure, including certain stock price levels. Such "golden leashes," as they are called, increase the risk that the director is beholden to the sponsor.

In addition, a payout based on stock price could influence important business judgments, such as optimal borrowing levels and whether to make or accept acquisition offers. For these reasons, special bonuses for certain directors risks creating board factions and infighting.

Second, when directors are appointed as the result of a settlement, outside normal governance procedures, the other shareholders did not get a vote. Such arrangements can lead to board members who appeal unduly to the activist and incumbents.

One solution to this problem is to put a settlement to a vote by the other shareholders.[2] This would assure appointment of directors with consensus support, as well as validate any other aspects of the settlement, such as committee assignments, director removal, terms and term limits, and corporate governance guidelines.

Finally, incumbent managers or directors are seldom eager to have activist nominees join the board. When they do, frictions are common and, even among the most conscientious directors, harmony elusive.

Formulaic Selection

Indexers seldom nominate directors. In fact, during the past five years, none of the largest three indexers—which own enormous swaths of corporations worldwide—have formally nominated a single director to any public company board.[3]

Large indexers adopt their own guidelines stating general criteria for selection and voting, while others consult the similar guidelines produced by proxy advisers. Index proponents repeatedly express their view that popular governance reform features are good for most companies across a portfolio, not necessarily for all.[4]

Consider the approach of the leading proxy adviser, Institutional Shareholder Services (ISS). ISS opens its discussion of the board of directors not with statements of competence or corporate stewardship, but with "four fundamental principles [that] apply when determining votes on director nominees."

These are enumerated as independence, composition, responsiveness, and accountability. Only the assessment of "responsiveness" tends to be contextual—a statement of voting "case by base."

On independence, ISS makes three prescriptions: (1) a majority of directors must be independent; (2) the board must have three standing committees operating under formal charters and staffed only with independent directors—audit, compensation, and nominating; and (3) there must either be a lead independent director or an independent chairperson (not also serving as an executive officer).

Many such rules have become commonly accepted in recent decades, but the empirical evidence on their economic value remains inconclusive.[5] While the prescribed committees and their functions are required by federal law or stock exchange rules, director expertise is often of even greater value than independence. Unmentioned by the indexers are valuable alternatives such as committees on capital allocation or investment—as described in chapter 9.

While indexers support a rule splitting the chair and CEO roles, this is not always desirable. The theory is that boards elect and oversee the CEO, so having one person wear both hats creates a conflict. Yet that is only one vote among boards with many independent directors, so any conflict can easily be neutralized.

Many corporations thrive when led by an outstanding person serving as both chairperson and chief executive, just as others have failed when the roles are split—such as at Enron. Companies are about evenly divided on the practice: about half the S&P 500 splits the functions, while the other half combines them. QSs appear to think about this case by case and, if anything, slightly favor companies that combine rather than split the functions.[6]

On composition, ISS again states three rules: (1) directors should have diverse skills that add value to the board, rather than duplicating backgrounds from particular viewpoints, ideally illustrated in a graphical skills matrix; (2) regular meeting attendance is expected, defined as at least 75 percent of meetings of the full board and committees; and (3) attention is expected, determined by caps on the number of public company boards individual directors may serve—five in general or two for CEOs.

Critics challenge these composition directives as intrusive and formulaic. Taking items 2 and 3 first, attendance and attention are clearly necessary, but not sufficient, to determine a valuable board member. Rules of thumb are useful, but that's not how these rules operate. That is why the board of directors' sections of so many corporate websites portray check marks ticking off all the governance formulas that major indexers and proxy advisers champion.

While it is prudent to be concerned about directors stretching themselves too thin, an artificial definition, such as a maximum of two or five boards, is arbitrary and bound to miss the mark. After all, outstanding directors with no other occupation can almost certainly handle more than six, while the least conscientious busy professional might find one too much.

On accountability, ISS calls for regular director elections, opposes staggered terms, and believes in shareholder removal power, with or without cause. But state corporate law permits all these and many other approaches to director election and removal and leaves it to companies to choose those best suited for their circumstances.

Concerning staggered boards, proponents stress advantages such as continuity and institutional knowledge, while critics cite insulation from accountability. But answers to such issues require context. Some evidence indicates that staggered boards add value.[7] Companies continue to be divided on the right approach.[8] What's clear is that ISS favors regimentation over context on this issue and many others where QSs prefer a contextual approach.[9]

Just as major indexers do not nominate directors, they rarely initiate shareholder proposals. For instance, their guidelines express a preference for annual director elections rather than for staggered board terms. While indexers often support related proposals by other shareholders, the largest among them have never put forth their own proposals to make such a change.[10]

Defenders of indexers urge deference to their relative intervention, saying their vast economies of scale warrant presuming that their decisions are in the best interests of their investors.[11] Critics of indexers say these practices show they are beholden to management.[12] Still others chalk this up to "rational reticence": proponents incur all costs of proposals but gain a fraction of the payoff, so it is rational to free ride by supporting others without taking the lead.[13]

The notion of rational reticence may be reinforced by a further possibility: the guidelines reflect "best practices" that are *probably desirable for most*, while indexer inaction reflects that such practices are *certainly undesirable for some*. If indexers lack resources to determine what is best in given cases, the rational strategy may be to avoid taking the initiative but to support others who do so.

Transients

Investors with holding periods less than one year cast votes in annual elections despite the fact that they will not continue to be shareholders for the directors' full terms. Even investors with holding periods less than two or three years who cast votes in electing staggered boards will not be around for as long as the directors they elect.

Transients have a short-term outlook. They may prefer directors who are likeliest to make decisions that will most immediately result in higher stock prices or cash distributions.

Gender Diversity

Gender diversity is among the hot-button issues in corporate governance today. Views on this subject do not appear to be influenced by shareholder cohort—proponents and skeptics alike appear among all the cohorts. Disagreements instead appear to be based on different views as a matter of sociology, politics, and data. Nevertheless, such a hot topic warrants attention, and it is worth pointing out that, on balance, it appears that QSs favor this movement.

Everyone can agree on the observed data of female underrepresentation on corporate boards compared to the population. Among public company directors in Canada and the United States, about 25 percent are women, up from 10 percent a decade ago.[14] Despite agreement on those points, however, people view the rate of change differently—some say such progress is too slow and urge moving more rapidly.[15]

Disagreement rages on the causes of underrepresentation. Among alleged and disputed causes: within corporations, a lack of prioritization by boards and, externally, lack of interest among women; gender stereotypes or in-group bias; and underrepresentation of women in the relevant pool or pipeline (which may, in turn, reflect gender stereotypes and in-group biases). There is more widespread agreement on another cause: board seats turn over slowly in corporate life, on average less than one seat per board per year. But participants disagree, often vigorously, about whether companies should adopt policies to speed turnover.

One reason the rate of progress is slower than some desire is the mixed rationales for the quest. There are two broad potential rationales for board gender diversity: (1) the economic interests of corporations and their shareholders and/or (2) the social interests around intuitions of fairness, equality, or justice.[16]

Empirical academic research on whether board gender diversity improves corporate economic performance is equivocal.[17] True, many studies find a positive association between gender diversity and corporate performance, but almost no empirical academic research finds any causation. Stanford University's Deborah Rhode and Amanda Packel conducted a comprehensive review of the empirical literature on the effects of gender diversity—and other forms of cultural diversity such as race—on corporate economic performance. Packel summarized the results:

> A full review of the empirical evidence reveals inconclusive results that are highly dependent on methodology and the specific measures of financial performance. While some studies have found positive correlations between representation of women on boards and various measures of company performance, others have found the opposite or no significant relationship. Moreover, correlations do not demonstrate causation. It could be that better firm performance leads to increased board diversity rather than the reverse, or that some omitted factors are affecting both board diversity and firm performance.[18]

Testing the effects of gender diversity on economic performance is complicated by the variety of relevant contexts to consider—such as board and company size, geography, or industry—as well as the variety of board settings, such as addressing acquisitions, dividends, executive performance and pay, financial reporting and auditing, or corporate culture and compliance. These challenges have long beset the parallel literature on the relation between director independence and corporate performance—which likewise does not support the view that independence contributes to superior performance.[19]

The social case is more compelling and is being forcefully made by many advocacy groups, which have made board gender diversity a top priority. Some focus almost exclusively on the subject, including 2020 Women on Boards in the United States and the 30% Club Canada. Others adopt it is as a tenet among a broader governance agenda, including the Canadian Coalition for Good Governance (CGG). In its report, *Building High Performance Boards*, CGG stresses that director quality is paramount, while also urging board diversity—in terms not just of gender but ethnic, cultural, and other personal characteristics of the corporation's various communities as well.

In late 2017, the 30% Club Canada began its campaign to achieve a minimum of 30 percent women on corporate boards. It explained that target as a critical mass where "contributions of a minority group cease being representative of that particular group and begin to be judged on their own merit." The group advocates disclosure, affirmative outreach, training, and commitment to "rigorous" board assessment and "regular board refreshment."

In the United States, the 2020 Women on Boards named itself for its goal: that by the year 2020, at least 20 percent of board seats would be held by women. It met this target by late 2019, when it announced that 20.4 percent of public company boards among the Russell 3000 were held by women.[20] The organization highlights the companies among that index boasting 20 percent or more female members—at last count a total of 176.[21]

There appears to be a positive association between gender diversity and QS density. For instance, 70 percent of the 2020 Women on Boards' honorees rank in the top half for QS density and 15 percent of honorees rank in the top decile. Such figures are consistent with other data indicating that gender diversity correlates to other positive outcomes. Table 11.1 presents some examples of 2020 honorees among the most successful in attracting QSs.

While the data on board gender diversity are not conclusive, in light of social arguments favoring gender diversity, there is a reliable intellectual basis for promoting board gender diversity.

Table 11.1
Board gender diversity and QS density

Alliant Energy	Johnson & Johnson
American Tower	Kaiser Aluminum
Arthur J. Gallagher & Co.	PepsiCo
Eli Lilly & Company	Stryker Corporation
Estée Lauder Companies	Sysco Corporation
International Flavors and Fragrances	

In doing so, of course, emphasis must remain on the quality profile of each director: formulaic governance remains unappealing.

In corporate governance, QSs care most about substance, the reasoning behind particular policies at specific companies. As a result, they tend to be averse to checklists prescribing "good governance." They prefer directors chosen on their merits, stressing business wisdom and capital allocation insight, rather than on checklists and formulas indexers use or representatives of particular constituencies, such as activists.

In governance, one size does not fit all. Further, many policies advocated under the banner of "good governance"—such as "board refreshment" and "corporate sustainability"—may be "good" in principle, but in practice are not necessarily best for a corporation or its shareholders. Likewise, experience and track record are more probative predictors of director contributions than benchmarks such as the number of other boards one serves on, tenure, age, or gender.

Indexers, in contrast, are concerned about the performance of a portfolio rather than particular companies, so they prescribe policies expected to benefit the overall market on average, not particular companies. Given the size and reach of the indexing segment, they have become a powerful force in the field of corporate governance.

Activists, while targeting more selectively, press for particular changes, not always for the best, and collective backgrounds and experiences.

QSs, of course, are aligned with a focus based solely on the company's long-term prosperity. Appealing to them are governance provisions that make sense for the particular company and directors who make decisions given the company's particular circumstances.

Electing directors and weighing in on occasional hot-button governance issues are among the most important powers a shareholder exercises. Therefore, variables and factors in shareholder voting are critical to the discussion, teed up in chapter 12.

12

Managerial Performance
The Overpaid and Underpaid

IN 1995, THE WALT DISNEY company wooed Michael Ovitz with a lavish employment contract. Ovitz, a prominent Hollywood figure and friend of CEO Michael Eisner, was appointed president. His contract provided for a lucrative payout, consisting dominantly of very short term stock options, if the company fired him without cause.

Fourteen months later, Disney did fire him without cause, triggering a payout of nearly $140 million. While the payout drew widespread public condemnation, courts upheld the contract. The courts deferred to the Disney board, while simultaneously recognizing that much of its work was perfunctory and far from best practices. To quote the Delaware Supreme Court:

> If measured in terms of the documentation that would have been generated if "best practices" had been followed, the record leaves much to be desired. . . . Despite its imperfections, . . . the compensation committee had adequately informed itself of

the potential magnitude of the entire severance package, including the options.[1]

Executive pay has long been a hot topic, drawing headlines for nearly a century. Most people are concerned with pay levels, especially relative to those of workers. A more important corporate concern, however, is whether pay aligns executive interests with a long-term time horizon, as vehemently favored by QSs.

Some pay aligns more with the short term, especially stock options; activists and transients rarely spotlight pay; and there is evidence that indexers are extremely passive in this area. Leading indexers believe the details are better resolved by boards and their consultants. While boards do have the ultimate burden, despite say on pay, they benefit from the attention that only QSs, among cohorts, offer on pay.

A little history and context will be useful before highlighting persistent trouble spots, along with contrasting overpaid and underpaid CEOs.

Historical Perspective

Public debate on executive compensation in America dates back to 1930. That year, public acrimony erupted after a profit-sharing plan yielded American Tobacco's chief executive an annual bonus of $850,000 when average wages were $2,000 and the unemployment rate nearly 20 percent.[2] (In today's dollars, that bonus would approximate $12 million.)

Still, modern corporations have long recognized the appeal of awarding bonuses as part of executive compensation to motivate desired performance. Among the first was Bethlehem Steel in 1902. Such plans, as well as profit-sharing, became common in the interwar period, with nearly two-thirds of public companies adopting them by 1928.

In recent history, public policies have favored "performance-based pay," also known as bonuses. For instance, in the 1970s, the threat of the Nixon administration's wage freezes, which exempted such pay, led corporations to enhance this component. On the other hand, the period's stagnating stock market induced a shift away from stock options in favor of bonuses based on non-market metrics such as long-term earnings growth.

In the 1980s, the hostile takeover era spawned change-of-control provisions called golden parachutes. Employment contracts called for companies to pay substantial sums to executives if they were forced to leave the company after another party gained control of it. The payouts were designed in part to deter unwanted bids for control, so they often yielded staggering sums. The effect was to help ratchet up executive pay levels. Excesses were exposed in Graef Crystal's 1991 book, *In Search of Excess.* (The title appeared to be a play on the title of another popular business book of the era, *In Search of Excellence.*)

Professor Crystal, a longtime executive compensation consultant, accurately portrayed the era's prevailing process: the CEO, after consulting with a compensation expert, laid out a proposed pay package, and the board of directors approved it. Many boards enlisted compensation committees to conduct formal negotiations with the chief, but those directors mostly lacked requisite expertise and rarely retained their own consultants to supply it. Plus, back then, CEOs tended to handpick directors and shape their own pay scales too.

Public outcry over the excess led the SEC in 1992 to require more extensive pay disclosure in proxy statements. After all, disclosure can be a strong disinfectant, as Justice Louis Brandeis noted. In many cases, however, this move backfired. When CEOs saw rivals making more than they did, compensation committees were asked to redress the slight. In such cases, disclosure pumped pay up rather than tamping it down.

Congress used the tax code, limiting the deductibility of executive pay that was not based on performance. Along with a period of record profits and rising stock prices, the legislation encouraged greater use of stock options. The combination of rising stock prices and incentives to pay executives in stock helped to drive executive pay skyward. Public criticism grew in tandem.

In the early 2000s, after the stock market bubble burst and a dozen major corporate accounting frauds were exposed, shareholders demanded change and boards stiffened their spines. Oversight was beefed up in both the Sarbanes-Oxley Act and stock exchange rules. Yet despite such change, by 2005, a number of companies were discovered to be manipulating stock option grants, backdating some to make them profitable and issuing others on the eve of news calculated to drive stock price up.

These practices were uncovered by a finance professor at the University of Iowa, Erik Lie. He found statistical anomalies among option grants, stock prices, and paydays.[3] Professor Lie put his findings succinctly:

> This study documents that the abnormal stock returns are negative before unscheduled executive option awards and positive afterward. The return pattern has intensified over time, suggesting that executives have gradually become more effective at timing awards to their advantage. . . . Unless executives possess an extraordinary ability to forecast the future market wide movements that drive these predicted returns, the results suggest that at least some of the awards are timed retroactively.

The SEC and Justice Department opened investigations on more than one hundred companies. These led many to restate their financials; a few dozen executives were fired; a dozen convicted of crimes; and a half dozen went to jail. It turned out, however, that the practice, while almost always unethical, was not always illegal. The result added to public cynicism around executive pay.

To adapt Michael Kinsley's quip about Washington, "The scandal isn't what's illegal, the scandal is what's legal."

The 2008 financial crisis revealed that some incentive compensation programs were extremely asymmetrical. Executive pay should be designed to apportion rewards and penalties in relation to risk—big rewards for manager and company alike on the upside but proportional losses for both on the downside. Ahead of the financial crisis, however, many executive pay plans gave managers huge gains when bets played out but inflicted no losses when they did not. Credit markets failed, in part, because managers took huge gambles, as there was huge possibility for upside and limited downside to their pay.

Amid deteriorating financial conditions, the U.S. government provided extensive and unorthodox financial support for many, such as supporting the acquisition by an insurance company (the Hartford) of a small ($10 million) bank to make it eligible for a loan (in that case, $3.4 billion).[4]

As a condition to this support, legislation required the government to impose limits on the form and amount of compensation to senior executive officers.[5] A subsequent audit of the government's compliance with the legislation revealed only partial enforcement, as the government demonstrated greater interest in being repaid than in limiting executive pay.[6]

A further round of regulatory oversight followed on three fronts. First, stock exchange rules require independent board compensation committees to set pay and disclose related policy. Second, companies must disclose the ratio of top executive pay to that of the median employee. And at least every three years, companies must hold formal shareholder votes on pay—and ask shareholders every six years whether to make those votes more or less frequent. These are only advisory votes, not binding, and of uncertain effect, so they are better classified as a signal on pay (not, as the popular but misleading slogan has it, say on pay).

It is therefore left to boards of directors to set and review executive compensation. Along with choosing a CEO, this may be the most important responsibility a board has. A few CEOs who consciously cultivate QSs make a point of receiving moderate salaries compared to peers. Don Graham is a leading example, as explained in a 2002 letter to shareholders of the Washington Post Co.:

President Bush said in a speech during 2002 that CEOs should report the total amount of their compensation in the chairman's letter. OK. When I became CEO in 1991, after consulting with some members of our board, I decided to freeze my compensation at the amount I had been receiving as publisher of *The Post*. I make $400,000 a year and participate in one company bonus plan which, if the company performs quite well, pays out a maximum to me of $400,000 every two years. I also receive some shares of restricted stock (300 shares in the most recent cycle) as part of the same plan. This hasn't changed in years.

When considering pay versus performance, some executives who consciously cultivate QSs often appear vastly underpaid. The following story comes from longtime concentrated Markel shareholder Mark Hughes of Lafayette Investments:

A few years ago, after the Markel annual meeting, I talked to two Board members about this and recommended increases in pay. I think this was a first in corporate America! To their credit, the Board members told me that they recognized this and once a few transitional changes were made, they intended to rectify the situation. In subsequent years, executive pay did increase and I think pay is more in line with where it should be. I think it is only appropriate that if shareholders complain about excessive pay, in the rare case where the opposite occurs, this should also be noted. You don't want to lose good people who might feel they are underappreciated.

Option Problems

Controversy over the level of stock option pay is intensified by debate on accounting for options. Before 2004, U.S. accounting standards treated stock option compensation as only the issuance of equity, recorded in the owners' equity section of the balance sheet, but not on the income statement. Many objected, arguing that managers had a duty to explain the real costs of option compensation even if accounting standards did not require it.[7] Critics finally persuaded the Financial Accounting Standards Board that stock options are a real economic cost and, since 2004, stock option expense must be listed on the income statement.

But how and when to measure the expense remains contestable. Option value fluctuates not only with such known factors as duration and exercise price but with such variables as interest rates, stock price volatility, and dividends. Today's accounting uses models incorporating these variables, though all agree they are imperfect and stock option expense is an estimate at best.

The other major issue concerns timing: accounting rules call for recording estimated option expense when issued rather than when exercised, though the latter is almost always vastly greater and represents the true economic cost. Critics believe managers have a duty to reveal the real cost, while accounting rules merely require what is often a fraction of that.

The critics have a point. At thousands of public companies, significant portions of corporate equity are being transferred from public shareholders to stock option recipients without being recorded. In the process, hidden incentives skew corporate decision making to favor option values over shareholder value, such as decisions on allocating capital to dividends versus buybacks, as discussed in chapter 11.

QSs believe that this largely hidden transfer of so much equity by options can have staggering implications. To recruit QSs, the best companies avoid stock options or report their cost faithfully.

Grant Advantages

While many companies offer executives outsized pay and upside-only stock options, incentives are better aligned if pay is rationally related to business performance, with no stock options. Compensation consultants generate fees by providing an intricate design for compensation packages. They work directly with executives on the assignment, even if nominally engaged by the board, and their interests will often align with those of the executives. Their value to the corporation and shareholders, therefore, is questionable.

In addition, consultants champion tying bonuses to stock prices, underestimating stock market risk. Stock price can deviate from intrinsic value due to many factors, from economic cycles to emotional trading. Stock price bubbles may reward the undeserving and crashes penalize the faithful.

Granting restricted stock units is a reasonable alternative. Companies agree to issue shares after the employee reaches a vesting period, such as employment for four years. Ideally, the bonus is a given amount of money, measured in shares by their trading prices at delivery. One appeal of this simple approach is the exact costs are clear, in contrast to the notoriously imprecise measure of stock option costs.

Above all, the key in all equity-related plans is to ensure that employees prosper when shareholders do and that employees suffer when shareholders do. Options do not satisfy this elementary requirement, while grants do.

The Underpaid and Overpaid

While critics of executive compensation harp on those at the top, with high ratios of pay to median workers, the other extreme garners too little attention. A few dozen CEOs have cut their salaries to essentially nothing—a mere nominal sum such as one dollar per year. Such a move attracts attention, but care should be taken to distinguish among different motivations and contexts.

There is an old American tradition of rich people serving the government as consultants for a nominal salary of $1. The practice stretches back to the early twentieth century, when civic-minded individuals helped run the government during wars, including famous names such as Bernard Baruch and today Mike Bloomberg and Mitt Romney.

A newer tradition has arisen of CEOs taking $1 salaries from their companies. But they do so for different reasons with different signification for QSs.

In one group are leaders of troubled companies attempting to send a signal of selfless commitment to recovery. Notable examples are Lee Iacocca at Chrysler in 1978 and Vikram Pandit at Citigroup in 2007. Another cohort has taken $1 cash salaries while concurrently receiving massive value in the form of stock options or other sources such as fees. Neither category is likely to attract investment interest from QSs.

A third category, however, are outstanding executives of prosperous companies who cut their salaries to nominal sums and take no other form of compensation either. While such a step is not remotely necessary to attract QSs, it is certainly a draw.

Research for this book revealed approximately 250 top executives among all SEC registrants drawing a nominal (typically $1) salary for at least one year over the past decade. The pool falls below thirty-five when limited to companies appearing on the annual entry at least five times. The smaller pool boasts a few companies scoring high in QS density, including Expedia, National Instruments, and Post Holdings. However, probably reflecting the many and varied reasons for joining the $1 club, the distribution of companies does not support concluding that nominal executive salaries are associated with higher QS densities.[8]

In fact, QSs generally believe in pay for performance. While it may be unseemly or unjust for CEOs of large public companies to draw nine-figure salaries when median worker pay is in the five figures, voluntary service is not required as long as senior executives earn their payday—by nurturing human capital while deploying financial capital at high rates of return.

Perhaps the most important barometer of executive pay rationality is what shareholders think. While say-on-pay votes are imperfect, nonbinding, and of little interest to indexers, activists, or transients, this is a place where QSs can make themselves heard. In fact, shareholder voting may be the most important topic in corporate life these days, as shareholders weigh in on more matters than ever with greater consequences, starting with pay.

The topic's importance can be seen in the many pending proposals to tweak long-standing shareholder voting rules. Chapter 13 reviews a series of these newly designed rules that would alternately deter activists, discourage transients, or disenfranchise indexers. To this series of proposals, this book's last chapter will add one: a newly designed voting regime that would reward QSs.

13

Shareholder Voting
One Each, Dual Class, or Quality?

IN RECENT BLOCKBUSTER PROXY BATTLES decided by thin margins—such as DuPont or Procter & Gamble—shareholders each had one vote per share. That's the conventional practice in shareholder voting, but not mandatory. If DuPont or Procter & Gamble had other voting rules, the companies might look very different today.

Suppose DuPont had two classes of stock, each with its own voting rights. In addition to potentially changing the outcome, this would certainly have widened the margin in favor of the class with more votes. Or suppose Procter & Gamble granted more votes to shares held for longer periods. Although the outcome may not have changed, the margin would, in favor of the more seasoned cohort.

Voting rules become more important as shareholders become increasingly fragmented and when there are more occasions to vote. With today's close votes on everything from say on pay to director elections—along with the specter of activism, the rising power of indexers, and continued concerns over short-termism—people have been exploring alternative voting regimes.

Dual-class structures draw headlines due to their use by prominent tech companies, and time-weighted voting is getting more attention, in part because of the political appeal of trashing short-termism. After canvassing several voting standards, I offer up in this chapter a novel approach: to increase the voting power of shares held not only for longer periods but in higher concentrations—empowering the QSs.

Dual Class

The baseline voting rule for most listed companies globally is one share–one vote. Long-standing, democratic, and rarely controversial, it is seen by many as the gold standard. But some companies have long believed it ill suited. They instead adopted dual-class structures, in which one class may have one vote per share but at least one other class has superior voting rights, such as ten per share.

The dual-class structure has been adopted by hundreds of companies, gaining popularity with tech companies in the past decade. Many companies launching an initial public offering (IPO) prefer dual-class structures and will list on the exchanges that allow it. In recent years, both Manchester United and Alibaba listed on the New York Stock Exchange—far away from home—solely for this reason.

The issue with dual-class capital structures is that they vest control in a group without matching economic risks: despite equal investments, one class has more votes per share than the other. The controlling class is insulated from short-term pressure but also from accountability. On the other hand, that controlling class may have a longer time horizon or business insight worthy of enhanced voting power.

The most dramatic instance began with the 1925 public offering of securities by Dodge Brothers Inc. The total market capitalization was $130 million and the investment banking firm Dillon,

Read & Co. took a $2.25 million stake. Because the shares Dillon, Read acquired carried multiple votes per share, it received majority voting control despite owning a minority economic interest.[1]

Oddly, people only took notice of the situation after an academic presentation given to the Academy of Political Science by Professor William Ripley in October 1925. Noting the Dodge offering almost in passing, he expressed concern about banks acquiring such outsized control at the expense of ordinary shareholders. He suggested the possibility of government regulation to prevent it.

Ripley's remarks ignited a firestorm, starting with press coverage the next day. The speech was widely reprinted—promptly in the *New York Times*, later in *Atlantic Monthly* and *Nation*, and finally in the *Congressional Record*.

Critical news stories and editorials followed. President Calvin Coolidge invited Professor Ripley to the White House to discuss the matter. The topic became a major issue of public concern, simmering alongside the economic populism that led to the first of many federal securities laws being enacted in 1933.[2]

The New York Stock Exchange banned dual-class stock, a ban that remained in effect through 1985. It granted a few waivers, with conditions, particularly when founders showed having special skills or vision warranting such enhanced power. For instance, in 1980 it listed Nike Inc., whose shares were identical except that those held by founder Phil Knight could elect three-quarters of the board. Knight said he would not have taken the company public otherwise.

Other exchanges, such as Nasdaq, also banned dual class subject to conditions such as a minimum portion of minority board seats, a maximum ratio of control shares to minority shares, and antidilution protections. Since the mid-1990s, the exchanges, while permitting IPOs with dual-class structures, forbid listed companies from going dual class. This ban occurred because many companies were making the switch to thwart hostile takeovers, often done coercively by placing high-vote/low-dividend stock with management, while dangling low-vote/high-dividend stock to outsiders.

While dual class remains lawful, leading index providers have begun to exclude companies with such structures from their indexes.[3] Today, some 250 companies maintain dual-class capital structures.[4] (Actually, quite a few have multiple classes of stock with varying voting rights, so they are "multiple-class" capital structures, but the phrase "dual class" is most commonly used to capture all variations.)

Resurgent interest in dual-class IPOs began in the mid-2000s as the tech sector rallied. Debate came to focus on duration: people could accept the structure as long as it wasn't permanent. The question being asked was: how long would the dual-class terms endure and under what circumstances might they cease? Before 2000, nearly two-thirds of dual-class offerings had no sunset provisions. But expiration terms have become common, whether at fixed times such as five to ten years or upon events such as the founder's death or incapacity.[5]

Founders argue that they need to retain the voting power to protect their companies from intense, short-sighted pressure from the public shareholders. The reasoning follows, however, that the founder's "special sauce" offers initial value, but tends to fade with time and depends on personal engagement. Knight's vision may have been vital to Nike's early years, but others took it successfully from there (though its dual-class structure continues). While critics worry that the structures insulate companies from market discipline or shareholder oversight, the evidence is uncertain. In any event, few dual-class structures created decades ago endure: the companies having rescinded them or been sold or dissolved.

A resurgence of dual-class structures appeared in 2017, especially among technology companies. Distinct was the IPO of Snap Inc., whose public shares carried no voting rights. Many observers fulminated. Some campaigned for the SEC or stock exchanges to crack down on the practice. While authorities refrained from doing so, advocates found redemption when compilers of certain market indexes barred newly created dual-class companies from inclusion. A sense of outrage accompanied some reports, such as this from the Council of Institutional Investors (CII):

> Following the egregious no-vote IPO of Snap Inc. and requests by CII and other concerned investor groups, three major index providers opened public consultations on their treatment of no-vote and multi-class structures. The FTSE Russell consultation resulted in a decision to exclude past and future developed market constituents whose free float constitutes less than 5 percent of total voting power. S&P Dow Jones' consultation resulted in a broader, but only forward-looking exclusion, which bars the addition of multi-class constituents to the S&P Composite 1500 index and its components, covering the S&P 500, MidCap 400 and SmallCap 600 indexes.

The CII reports that the exclusion had moderate effects.[6] The number and percentage of newly listed companies with dual-class capital structures did not immediately change dramatically—19 percent, 11 percent, and 26 percent in 2017, 2018, and 2019 (through first half), respectively—though the total market capitalization of such companies has fallen substantially—49 percent, 17 percent, and 15 percent, respectively. The frequency and duration of sunset provisions had not moved much either—about one-fifth of new dual-class structures continue to have sunsets, typically after ten years, though CII recommends seven. Amid the controversy, therefore, it's clear that many companies prefer the advantages of dual class to the advantages of being included in stock market indexes.

After all, categorical condemnation of dual-class capital structures ignores their utility in specific scenarios.[7] Adopters include family companies (such as Tootsie Roll Industries); entrepreneur firms (such as Tillys); and those whose industries demand a long-term focus, such as journalism (New York Times Co.), spirits (Brown-Forman), and finance (Houlihan Lokey). Many dual-class structures have plain vanilla terms—more votes on all matters to one class than another, including some fifty companies within the Russell 3000 that have at least one class of stock without any voting rights.[8]

The terms of dual-class structures vary widely. About fifteen companies use complex formulas to allocate corporate power and another fifteen provide for specific allocations of board seats, some by number of slots and others by percentage (such as Nike). For instance, at Forest City Realty Trust, Graham Holdings, Madison Square Garden, and Scholastic, one class is entitled to elect a majority of the board, typically two-thirds, while another can elect the rest.

In some cases, such as with the Boston Beer Company, the approach to board elections by class appears designed to protect minority interests by granting minority shareholders greater voting power. Several dual-class structures adjust the voting rules on extraordinary matters such as mergers, either reducing the super-voting shares to one vote or increasing the other class to one vote, including at News Corp., Sinclair Broadcast, Sonic Automotive, and Virtu Financial.

In a final illustration of the variety of approaches to voting rules, some limit rather than expand the power of large majorities. For example, McCormick & Co. has two classes of stock, one voting, one nonvoting; but its charter also provides that when a single owner commands at least 10 percent of the vote, its shares beyond those amounting to 10 percent are not entitled to any vote. Similarly, at United Parcel Service, which has three classes entitled to different voting rights, if a stockholder controls 25 percent of a given vote, every additional share beyond that is entitled only to one-thousandth of a vote per share.

Given the wide variety of approaches to shareholder voting, QSs examine dual-class structures on a case-by-case basis. Among companies with dual-class structures are a substantial cohort with high QS density.[9] Table 13.1 is a sampling of dual-class companies ranking in the top quartile in terms of attracting QS.

Table 13.1
Dual-class capital structures and QS density

Aflac	Graham Holdings
Berkshire Hathaway	Hershey Company
Brown-Forman	Hyatt Hotels
Constellation Brands	McCormick & Co.
Discovery Communications	Moog
Dish Network	New York Times Co.
Erie Indemnity	Nike
Estée Lauder Companies	United Parcel Service
Expedia	John Wiley & Sons

Time-Weighted Voting

If the chief argument for dual-class shares is that they pair voting power to vintage, there is a more direct way to do that using time-weighted voting. Time-weighted voting prescribes that a share's voting power is increased after it has been held for a given number of years. A common approach grants four votes instead of one to each share held longer than four years. When those shares are sold, they revert back to one-vote shares.

Designs vary to suit, with differences in the definitions of short and long term (upping votes after three, five, or ten years say), reward increments (adding one vote per two years or two votes per one year), and matters covered (all matters coming to a vote or only designated matters such as mergers). In theory, by rewarding long-term ownership, average holding periods should rise and stock volatility fall.

From the shareholders' viewpoint, time-weighted voting remains democratic. All shares and shareholders enjoy identical opportunities to gain enhanced voting rights. The chief criticism

of time-weighted voting is that holding period length is an imperfect proxy for wisdom or good judgment.

Reasonable people can disagree on whether the resulting concentration of power in the longer-term shareholders is superior.
If the long-term shareholders are indexers with insufficient interest
in particular companies, while the newer shareholders are prepared to engage productively, time-weighted voting backfires.[10]

To illustrate, imagine a simple shareholder base, where the
period of ownership of outstanding shares is about equally distributed among older and newer shareholders and those in between—
such as 33 percent own for less than one year, more than three
years, and in between.

With ninety-nine shares outstanding, each cohort controls
thirty-three votes. No single cohort can command the outcome of
any vote. But if time-weighted voting added three votes to each
share held longer than three years, then that cohort would have
ninety-nine votes, the others would still have thirty-three each and
a combined sixty-six. The seasoned cohort would then dictate the
outcome of every vote. But it is not obvious that such seasoning
translates into proportionally greater wisdom for a company.

Empirical evidence on the effects of time-weighted voting
is limited.[11] Only a handful of U.S. companies currently maintain time-weighted voting: Aflac, Carlisle, J.M. Smucker, Quaker
Chemical, and Synovus Financial. A few others once employed
time-weighted voting but have since rescinded it, including Church
& Dwight, Cincinnati Milacron, Roper Technologies, and Shaw
Group.[12] Despite the small sample size, all such companies that
have experimented with time-weighted voting rank high in terms
of attracting QSs.[13]

Many listed French companies have also used time-weighted
voting, with a two-year minimum holding period, including half
the CAC-40. In fact, in 2014 French lawmakers made time-
weighted voting the default for listed French companies, unless
shareholders vote to opt out of it.

Early empirical results suggest considerable value associated with time-weighted voting—called loyalty shares in France.[14] Companies opting out of loyalty shares suffered a negative market reaction, while those adhering to time-weighted voting enjoyed a positive market reaction. The theory? Loyalty shares encourage costly monitoring by long-term shareholders, providing potential benefits to all shareholders. While the 2014 start date makes the French experiment a new one, it clarifies another point: administrative and compliance burdens can be handled.

Outside France, however, more time is needed to produce useful empirical data on how time-weighted voting plays out, including whether it lengthens overall time horizons of a company's shareholder base. Researchers who have crunched the data document that time-weighted voting rewards inside ownership and benefits smaller outside owners.[15] They encourage further experimentation with how corporate voting might shape individual companies and influence financial markets.

A number of experimental alternatives have recently been proposed.

Novel Approaches

One proposal would be for index funds to abstain from voting altogether—contrary to current law, which requires large institutional investors to cast their ballots.[16] The effect would increase the voting power of QSs as well as all non-indexers. Such a rule, however, would face political resistance, and most commentators who have studied the proposal have declined to back it.[17]

An alternative would call for indexers to pass voting power through to ultimate beneficiaries—the customer account holders in the fund. While appealing, there are two drawbacks. First, administrative costs would be high. Second, gains are likely to be slight, as most individuals, the dominant account holders, fail to vote. (Economists call this *rational apathy*—for most individuals, the cost to become informed vastly outweighs the gain in value of small stakes.)

A third approach would compromise based on the type of voting topic: continue to let index funds vote on matters with which shareholder interests are likely to be aligned, such as mergers, while passing the vote to account holders on contestable topics, such as environmental issues.[18] While also appealing, this proposal faces the definitional challenge of classifying the type of voting topic as well as the same issue of rational apathy of the account holders.

One general problem with any proposal put forward is that implementation would require changes in the law. Given the political and uncertain nature of attempts to change legislation, it's more advantageous for companies to approach shareholder voting on terms the law currently permits. A broad range of lawful options exist.

As one example, boards may simply grant stock dividends to shareholders owning stock for designated periods or in specified amounts. Saudi Aramco took this approach after its initial public offering in late 2019, the largest ever at $2.5 trillion. All shareholders holding the stock for at least six months were granted additional shares. The purpose was to entice shareholders to continue to own the stock through the somewhat volatile period following this massive offering.

For another approach, some U.S. companies, and a far larger number of European ones, adopt scale-limited voting: one share–one vote, but with a cap on the voting power of shareholders commanding large blocks, such as 10, 20, or 30 percent. The tapering feature is also used in some dual-class structures to limit the voting power of the stronger shareholder class, as seen in the examples of McCormick and UPS. Another interesting way to taper voting power with rising economic interest is voting that increases only by the square-root of shares—one share–one vote, but one hundred shares–ten votes.[19]

While such experimentation continues and sparks debate, I'm offering up an additional proposal tied to this book's thesis:

increasing the voting power of shares based not only on duration, as under time-weighted voting, but on the holder's relative concentration in the particular company's stock. I call it "quality voting."

Quality Voting

Quality voting refines time-weighted voting to account not only for duration but conviction. That is, quality voting grants additional votes to shares owned for a long time in large stakes.

Stakes can be measured in many different ways, as best suits a company's particular circumstances. An obvious choice would be the percentage of a shareholder's portfolio in the stock. Some companies might wish to use the measures created by researchers who track QSs. One of the proxies for investor conviction is a portfolio with a high concentration in the stock of a particular company.

Two votes per share could be granted to shareholders allocating between 1 percent and 5 percent of their portfolios to the company and three votes per share to those allocating more than 5 percent. If time-weighted voting implicitly assumes that longer-held shares cast higher-quality votes, the hypothesis follows that shares owned by those with greater exposure will also have such merit.

To adjust the previous illustration, suppose portfolio concentration is randomly distributed across durations. Combining duration with concentration, the short-term and unconcentrated cohort would remain entitled to thirty-three votes, while the longest holding and most concentrated would enjoy 199 votes. Updating table 13.2, which showed the effects of duration in time-weighted voting, table 13.3 adds the effects concentration.

The outcome of any vote would be determined by a fluid combination of shareholders boasting relatively longer durations and higher concentrations. To complete the illustration, table 13.4 applies the multiples to the previous example of a company with

Table 13.2
Time-weighted voting power

Duration and multiple	Normal votes	Time-weighted votes
< 1 year = 1×	33	1× = 33
1–3 years = 1×	33	1× = 33
> 3 years = 3×	33	3× = 99

Table 13.3
Quality voting power

	Duration multiple	Concentration multiple
None	< 1 year = no multiple	< 1% = no multiple
Some	1–3 years = 2×	1%–5% = 2×
Substantial	> 3 years = 3×	> 10% = 3×

Table 13.4
Votes given combinations of concentration and duration

Concentration/Duration	< 1% = no multiple	1%–5% = 2×	> 5% = 3×
< 1 year = no multiple	33	66	99
1–3 years = 2×	66	132	165
>3 years = 3×	99	165	198

Note: Shared area reflects number of votes commanded given concentration and duration levels.

ninety-nine shares outstanding, with thirty-three each held for varying durations and concentrations. (This example presents the multiples in the proportion of 1–2–3. That is a high magnitude of change in multiples, which may be too large for comfort in an experimental stage. More modest multiples could be set, such as 1, 1.33, 1.66, or even 1, 1.2, 1.4.)

One compelling advantage of quality voting: companies can adopt and tailor it without any changes in the law or regulatory approvals. Another: companies can design the details and tailor the arrangements to suit in a joint exercise involving solely board and shareholder approval. Each company must weigh the following costs and benefits of adoption.

Administrative burdens may be high. One problem is how most U.S. equity is held in the names of depository nominees rather than ultimate owners, complicating the task of tracking ownership concentration. Record-keeping and calculations can be complex, especially for large institutions investing through multiple funds, including those with diverse mixes of debt, equity, and other securities.

In fact, companies that rescinded time-weighted voting often cited administrative complexity as a reason. Administering commitment-weighted voting would pose additional cost, particularly in record-keeping and verification. For example, duration is a fixed measure of time, whereas concentration can vary substantially over time.

On the other hand, holdings are readily observable from public filings for institutional investors and can be verified by reference to disclosure that is legally required and subject to federal anti-fraud rules. For these shareholders, enhanced voting power could be made optional and subject to the company's confirmation of verified shareholder applications.[20]

Such a simple approach can be implemented immediately for all shareholders, including individuals, by shifting the burden of disclosure to the shareholder: any shareholder wishing to exercise quality shares would be required to submit qualifying evidence to the corporate secretary accordingly. The secretary can create uniform rules describing what evidence qualifies and standardized procedures to verify it.

Longer term, the challenges of administration are likely to be diminished greatly by automated approaches. Advances in tracking technology, particularly digital ledgers based on blockchain tools, promise to make administration of quality voting manageable. State corporate law now authorizes such approaches to maintaining shareholder lists, and some companies, led by Overstock.com, have begun to adopt them.

Under quality voting, activist shareholders may often gain enhanced power when they hold meaningful stakes for long periods. Voting power could also increase during the course of multiyear campaigns, as more votes accrue over time. Both points may attract activists, but while managers may see some associated costs, those activists will be more patient and focused than other shareholders, producing comparative gains.

Shareholders today vote on more matters than ever before. Their voice is more influential than ever. Yet they may have different interests. This explains the proliferation of alternative voting arrangements. Given research indicating the value to investors of committed long-term ownership and the potential power of quality voting, more companies ought to experiment with the quality voting approach.

Getting Indexers and
Activists Going Quality

THIS BOOK MAY HAVE BEEN written in the nick of time. Indexers are dominating corporate America. Technological innovation, especially AI, is propagating transience. Activists are becoming more influential. Amid the rise of all three of these shareholder cohorts over recent decades, QSs are a shrinking group. But their time is now.

No shareholder group can deny the essential functions QSs play: sounding board, constructive critic, champion of the long term, and ultimate arbiter of capital allocation and business value. Even devotees of indexing appreciate this role and are confident that indexing will never preempt such activities.[1] The most ardent proponents of activists appreciate that they cannot alone supply required accountability.[2] Those who question whether short-termism is a significant problem do so chiefly by emphasizing the presence of substantial long-term owners.

The best hope, moreover, may simply be to broaden the book's reach beyond QSs and those interested in attracting them, to include indexers and activists and maybe even transients. After all, indexers have enormous power. With even a modest increase in resources allocated to the attention of QS topics, they could be a huge positive force in corporate America. Rather than relying on generic governance guidelines and passive control, they would attend annual meetings, read annual letters, participate in engagement, understand capital allocation, and help identify and support quality directors.

Many activists already embrace these principles—in fact, many activists are QSs and some QSs are activists. The book's message will resonate with them and ideally entice other activists to take a few pages from it. For that matter, worth emphasizing is that few shareholders are purely members of one cohort at all times. Even most of the largest indexers are families of funds that also offer funds managed as QSs; even the largest QS families offer some indexed alternatives. There are active trading desks and rapid-fire arbs at many of the best QSs.

The bottom line: the QS cohort brings enormous value to companies and fellow shareholders alike, as well as markets generally.[3] Corporate managers are likely to continue to get the shareholders they deserve, and most deserve a high density of QSs.

APPENDIX A

Research, Method, and Names

QSS ARE FOND OF THE adage, attributed to John Maynard Keynes, that it is better to be approximately right than precisely wrong. This wisdom applies to any attempt to identify the QSs from among today's vast universe of institutional investors. Reliable selections must depend on both objective criteria and subjective calls. The following is a summary of the approaches used in this book, including detailed notes on the original empirical research conducted.

To repeat the simple selection criteria and challenge stated in the prologue, in hunting QSs and their investees, research was oriented toward identifying:

1. shareholders that historically, over a multiyear period, have exhibited a consistent behavior of investing in high concentrations and for long holding periods; and
2. companies whose shareholder base is composed of a high relative density of such shareholders.

The job is easier to state than execute, however, as there are many reasonable alternative approaches to measuring such features, all involving considerable judgment. Identifying QSs, for instance, poses alternative ways to calculate horizon (such as average holding periods or average portfolio turnover) and concentration (such as deviation from an index or number of positions in a portfolio). Choices must also be made in establishing relevant time spans of interest, say, one, three, or five years, and breakpoints, such as top quintile or quartile. Anomalies also need addressing, such as shareholders who combine concentrated long-term stockholdings with some indexing.

Identifying companies prone to attract such shareholders can be done by examining the respective shareholders' portfolios, individually and in aggregate. One inherent problem—besides being laborious—is distinguishing specific shareholder–company relationships, as some shareholders ranking high generally for duration and concentration might nevertheless be both fleeting and thin in given companies and vice versa—some investors generally operating short term with small stakes might hold some companies forever in outsized portions.

Companies might alternatively be identified more directly. For instance, one proxy for shareholder patience at given companies could be low share turnover. This can be measured either as shares traded compared to shares outstanding or dollar volume compared to market capitalization. Resulting shareholder lists could be used to identify each company's longest-term and largest holders.

However, share turnover overlooks the distribution of shareholders, so radically different bases could have identical share turnover. Contrast, for instance, one company's base composed entirely of shareholders of average patience versus another's containing half extremely patient and half extremely impatient shareholders. On the other hand, combining share turnover with average holding periods enables estimating the percentage of shares that are high or low turnover. Further probing could examine the portion of shareholders who sold 100 percent of their shares in a given year.

Statistics aside, the cohort of QSs is known by experience and reputation. Readers can probably reel off a list of quite a few such investors. In fact, managers and investors alike may also appreciate, as a matter of common sense, what policies and practices appeal to such investors. Yet intuition alone may be suspect— posing behavioral problems such as saliency bias as well as surprising variations between what we think and what is true. The best approach is therefore a combination of data and intuition, both rules-bound and principles-based decision making.

Thankfully, the exercise is more straightforward for a particular company. Each faces a concrete context, including an existing shareholder base, along with a specific history and goals. Those particulars can inform what sorts of shareholders are desirable to attract and which are plausible to cultivate. Indeed, they can also inform what corporate policies may appeal to such shareholders and which work for a particular company.

Original Empirical Research

Original empirical research in the hunt for QSs began by applying an inverse approach, in which we first segmented the universe of potential investee stocks and then segmented the highest QSs in that subuniverse. For the universe of stocks, after first removing small and unseasoned issuers (market caps less than $1.1 billion and less than nine quarters of data), we selected for institutional interest and financial performance, as described below. From among that subuniverse of companies, we identified those institutional investors with the highest concentration and conviction in their positions as well the greatest patience and longevity, using a multifactor ranking model, described later. For convenience, the result, 2,070 companies, is cited as Cunningham, QS Density Ranking.

Company Appeal

Quality. A purely quantitative measure of the relative quarterly rank of the stock to the universe was created using a weighted sum of four factors: (1) performance—such as risk-adjusted Sharpe and Sortino ratios, return on equity, and return on invested capital; (2) riskiness—volatility, downside deviation, ratio of negative returning months, and maximum drawdown (one, three, and five years); (3) upside capture—the ratio of months with positive returns and percentage of times the stock outperformed its annual expected return; and (4) turnover—trading volume as a multiple of outstanding shares (quarterly and annually).

Institutionality. The stock's institutional ownership structure was ranked based on four factors: (1) institutional breadth—the number of reporting institutional investors owning the stock (to manage the data, with some cost in size skewing, we limited this to those with at least $1 billion AUM); (2) institutional concentration—the average percentage ownership of each institution and the stock's institutional Herfindahl–Hirschman Index (HH Index); (3) institutional attractiveness—the cumulative institutional weight of the outstanding shares and voting percentage of institutional investors; and (4) institutional turnover—the level of institutional trading in the stock and percentage traded by institutions in a given quarter and year.

Analysis. For each metric, stocks were ranked from highest (100) to lowest (1) quarterly. The quarterly rank measures the stock's quarterly position versus the universe, calculated as the average sum of the foregoing eight metric ranks that quarter.

The stock's overall rank is the sum of the twenty quarterly ranks. The stock with the highest overall rank leads the list of stocks over the five-year window.

Shareholder Concentration and Conviction Factors

Portfolio Market Share. The percentage weight of the portfolio in its underlying market, computed by dividing the quarterly portfolio AUM by the aggregate market capitalization of all stocks it is invested in. A high market share can mean: (1) a relatively large AUM for a given number of stocks; (2) a relatively small number of stocks for a given AUM level; or (3) a relatively high concentration in large companies for a given AUM and number of stocks. A higher portfolio market share implies concentration and control on the investees of the portfolio. Higher ranks are assigned to greater portfolio market shares.

Portfolio Conviction. A compound equation drawing on three submetrics: (1) the average voting power of the portfolio in the companies of the stocks it holds; (2) number of stocks in the portfolio with significant ownership (0.1 percent or more of market cap); and (3) the total number of stocks in the portfolio. Portfolio conviction measures the portfolio manager's belief in and dedication to its underlying holdings, computed as the product of (1) the portfolio's average voting power and the percentage of stocks held with significant ownership (2 and 3). Higher ranks are assigned to greater portfolio conviction.

Portfolio Concentration. The relative concentration levels of the portfolio versus the universe of managers, computed as the product of the portfolio market share, average AUM per stock, and percentage of stocks held with significant ownership. The higher the value, the higher the portfolio concentration rank.

Portfolio Impact. The potential power the portfolio can exert on the companies whose stock it owns or the broader market, computed as the product of the portfolio market share, AUM per stock, and voting percentage. In relative terms, the higher the product of these three standardized measures, the greater the portfolio impact. Portfolio impact is constructed as two separate matrices, whose average provides the portfolio impact rank.

Portfolio Holdings Quality. Using the ranked list of stocks produced in our stock analysis step (described later), this measures the portfolio's concentration in the top quintile of stocks. Portfolio holdings quality is the product of the percentage weight of the portfolio's top quintile stocks and the average ownership percentage of the portfolio in those stocks. The greater the portfolio holdings quality, the higher the portfolio rank.

Shareholder Patience and Longevity Factors

Trade Noise. The ratio of the portfolio gross traded dollar value to its absolute net traded dollar value. A ratio of 1.00 is the minimum attainable, indicating that the net and gross traded values were identical. A ratio greater than 1.00 implies a less objective trading strategy. To refine the measurement, we multiply it by the number of portfolio trades in the quarter. A long term–oriented portfolio would have a lower turnover and fewer trades per quarter. A higher inverse rank indicates a more stable portfolio.

Portfolio Turnover. The ratio of the portfolio gross traded value dollar value to its AUM. Leveraged and trade-oriented portfolios have higher portfolio turnover, indicating a weaker quality-investing approach, and vice versa. Those with low portfolio turnovers receive higher rankings.

Turnover Impact. A measure of the impact of a portfolio's trading activity on its market, this is computed as the product of portfolio market share and portfolio turnover. A significant portfolio market share combined with high portfolio turnover could disrupt the overall investees' market and hence lower the quality of portfolio holdings, whereas a large portfolio market share with low portfolio turnover suggests a more stable market. Turnover impact identifies portfolios with large portfolio market share plus low portfolio turnover; by taking the inverse of this metric, the higher the rank, the more stable and impactful the portfolio is.

Portfolio Volatility. The rate of change and change magnitude of a portfolio's constituents, calculated by taking the periodic standard deviation and the overall standard deviation of stocks in the portfolio. Frequent changes indicate high trading activity and less-focused approach. Lower portfolio volatility values are ranked higher.

Shareholder Filters

Shareholders are screened as follows: (1) institutional investors registered and operating in the United States and/or Canada; (2) quarterly reporting during all quarters from 2014 to 2018; (3) minimum $1.1 billion AUM;[1] (4) majority of investments in corporate equity; and (5) removing avowed index funds, activists funds, and private equity funds.

Quality Shareholders

The twenty investors at the top of this list of QSs are as follows (in order down the columns):

Berkshire Hathaway	Blue Harbour	Lyrical
Gates Foundation	Baker Brothers	Viking Global
State Farm Auto Insurance	Temasek Holdings	Capital Research Global
Baupost Group	Scopia Capital	Matrix Capital
Fiduciary Management	Lone Pine Capital	Stockbridge Partners
Southeastern	Kensico Capital	Glenview Capital
	Cantillon Capital	Iridian Asset Management

Among their portfolio positions representing at least 2 percent of the portfolio, three hundred different stocks appeared. Of these, twenty appeared three times or more as listed below, and thirty-eight appeared twice (a selection of those also appears below):

Twice (a sampling)	Three times	Four times
Abbott Labs	Allergan	Alibaba
Accenture	Anthem	Thermo Fisher
Autodesk	Booking Holdings	United Health
Berkshire Hathaway	Broadcom	*Five times*
DowDuPont	Coca-Cola	Amazon
Ecolab	Constellation Brands	Visa
ExxonMobil	eBay	*Six times*
FedEx	Intel	Facebook
Investors Bank	Mastercard	Microsoft
Liberty Media	Netflix	*Nine times*
United Technologies	S&P Global	Alphabet (Google)
Walmart	TransDigm	

Supplemental Secondary Research

The original empirical research undergirding this book's discussion was supplemented and corroborated by a variety of secondary research.

Surveys. One way to identify QSs, in general or at particular companies, is to survey leading investors knowledgeable about the practices and histories of peers and rivals. A similar method for identifying companies as attracting quality would survey leading investor relations professionals with analogous knowledge.

The latter is an obvious winner for companies undertaking such an examination, whose in-house staff would be an excellent resource.

The survey approach is endorsed in several prominent writings by and about outstanding investors, heavily oriented toward QSs. Examples include the celebrated 1984 Buffett article, "The Superinvestors of Graham and Doddsville," and a 2005 sequel by Columbia University law professor Louis Lowenstein—along with a comment on the latter by Seth Klarman of Baupost Group, as well as many other books profiling outstanding investors.[2] Such research yields the following additional exemplars:

Brave Warrior	Phil Fisher	Ruane Cunniff
Chieftain	Glenn Greenberg	Lou Simpson
Davis Selected Advisers	Grinnell College	Southeastern
First Eagle	John Maynard Keynes	Tweedy, Browne
First Manhattan	Charlie Munger	Ralph Wanger
	Thomas Rowe Price	

Berkshire Based. Berkshire Hathaway's shareholder list is a good place to look for QSs. Start with the most concentrated Berkshire shareholders—there are at least 250 with more than 5 percent of their portfolio staked in the company, almost all of which have held the stock for decades. To make the search manageable and meaningful, select an appropriate sample or investment size, such as the twenty with the largest stakes or all those whose stakes exceed $250 million. Examine their portfolios to identify other companies they concentrate in for long periods. Finally, examine those companies to identify other concentrated long-term shareholders. The result will be a credible group of both

QSs and companies that attract them. Examples of concentrated and substantial long-term Berkshire shareholders:

Akre Capital	First Manhattan	Lourd Capital
Check Capital	Gardner, Russo & Gardner	Markel
Cortland Advisors	Giverny Capital	Ruane Cunniff
Davis Selected Advisers	Global Endowment	Wedgewood Partners
Douglass Winthrop	Greylin Investment	Weitz Investment
Eagle Capital	Kovitz	
Everett Harris	Lee, Danner & Bass	

Examples of other companies in which such Berkshire shareholders hold substantial long-term stakes:

Abbott Labs	Credit Acceptance	Markel
Accenture	Danaher	Nestlé
Alphabet (Google)	Fairfax Financial	O'Reilly Automotive
Amazon	Johnson & Johnson	Unilever
CarMax	Liberty Media	Wells Fargo
Constellation Software	Loews	

Trading Data. To proxy companies boasting patient shareholders, consider data relating either share trading volume to shares outstanding or dollar trading volume to market capitalization. I did the latter, using S&P Capital IQ data. We ran it for both smaller groups such as the S&P 500, larger groupings such as the Russell 3000, and even larger universes encompassing substantially all publicly traded companies. We examined results on different timelines: one, three, and five years. There was significant overlap in this step and the Berkshire-based approach. These are the thirty-nine companies from the S&P 500 with the lowest share turnover for the one-year period ending with the third quarter of 2018 (in order down the columns).

Berkshire Hathaway	Charles Schwab	Rollins
Alphabet (Google)	Stryker	Fortive
BlackRock	Northrop Grumman	Accenture
Johnson & Johnson	Wells Fargo	Ecolab
Coca-Cola	American Express	General Dynamics
Walmart	Union Pacific	Marsh & McLennan
Eli Lilly	ExxonMobil	PPG Industries
Pfizer	3M	Lockheed Martin
Abbott Labs	Roper Technologies	Bristol-Myers Squibb
Visa	Oracle Corporation	Microsoft
PNC Financial	JPMorgan Chase	Cisco Systems
Air Products	PepsiCo	Danaher
Procter & Gamble	UnitedHealth	Intuit Inc.

From among the Russell 3000, the following selected names appeared in the top quintile (in order down the columns):

Seaboard Corporation	Enstar	Graham Holdings
VICI Properties	Fairfax Financial	Liberty Global
Erie Indemnity	Markel	Alleghany
Brookfield Property	Constellation Software	Cimpress

Other Research. An obvious approach is to identify other published empirical research. For one, the research methods can be mimicked or adapted to suit particular companies by focusing on specific features such as size or industry. Such research rarely lists particular shareholders by type, instead analyzing aggregate data to address broader questions. But there are exceptions, such as a table of both QSs and transients in recent research about their different effects on given company risk profiles and market pricing.[3] The following chart presents each type (alphabetically).

Among top quality	Among top transients
Berkshire Hathaway	AIM
Capital Research & Management	Investors Research
Jennison Associates	Janus
Fidelity Management & Research	Putnam
Harris Associates (Oakmark Funds)	Marsico
State Farm	Oppenheimer
Southeastern Asset Management	UBS Warburg
Wellington	

Other Data. Leading researchers Cremers and Pareek created a 13F-based data set of all institutional investors dating to 1980, presenting, quarter by quarter, each shareholder's concentration (measured as deviation from the index, with the index equal to 0.0) and average holding period. In this massive database, the cutoffs for the top quintiles were 0.9 for concentration and 2.0 years for holding periods.[4] From the top quartile of both—excluding foundations and private equity funds holding one or a few stocks—choose a relevant time period, such as the most recent five years, omit duplicate names, and rank the remaining names by frequency of quarters making the list. Doing so yielded a total of 195 names, a rich vein of QSs. There was substantial overlap in this cohort with that identified using the other methods. Selected additional names follow (alphabetically):

Allen Holding	First Pacific	Timucuan
Bislett Management	Kahn Brothers	W. H. Reaves
Dane Falb Stone	Sleep, Zakaria & Co.	Wallace Capital
DF Dent	Southeastern	Water Street
Fenimore	Speece Thorson	Wintergreen Advisers
Fiduciary Management		

Other Resources. Several website services provide useful data for analysis. Rocket Financial digests quarterly updated 13F filings. The site presents resulting shareholder lists and investor portfolios in columns of data that can be sorted in a variety of ways and/or downloaded to spreadsheets for further manipulation, including calculating concentration. The site tabulates the quarterly filings over time in ways that enable calculating holding periods of interest as well.

The Floatspec website was made available to me during its incubation and before its developers sold it to PJT Partners. Their app does some such work for the user and presents results in summary form. Enter company or fund names, and the site presents brief profiles along with rankings, such as fund turnover and certain categories of shareholder type. One extract ranked shareholders by a combination of their quartile rankings in terms of turnover and concentration. There was substantial overlap in this cohort with that identified using both the Berkshire method and the previously discussed method. Selected additional names follow (alphabetically):

Aristotle Capital	Burgundy	Lee, Danner & Bass
Atlanta Investment	Douglass Winthrop	London Co. of VA
Barrow Hanley	Fairholme	Mar Vista
Beck, Mack & Oliver	Franklin Mutual	Sprucegrove
Broad Run	Greenbrier	Tweedy, Browne
Brown Brothers Harriman	Jackson National	

Self-Assertion. Yet another basis for identifying QSs is looking at what investors have to say about themselves and their styles and what they look for.

Company Focus. Each company can examine its own share-holder list to assess its mix of shareholders, whether indexers, transients, quality, or other. Changes in the shareholder base occurring around particular events—such as major acquisitions or executive successions—can be of special interest to reveal the variety of share-holder views and whether the events attracted or repelled particular shareholders and shareholder types. S&P Capital IQ data on public companies dating back to 2000 revealed useful insight for this book's discussions of evolution of the shareholder bases at the Washington Post Co. during its transition into Graham Holdings and at Leucadia through its merger into Jefferies.

Specific Levers. Concerning specific corporate policies or practices, we related existing publicly available data on various company practices to the QS Density Ranking of 2,070 companies based on their relative proportion of QSs (the "QSDR"). Results appear throughout the book.

For instance, we assess how a variety of specific company practices relate to the QSDR, including maintaining strong leadership in product branding, signing on to the Business Roundtable mission statement on corporate purpose, issuing dual-class stock, providing for very low (nominal) CEO pay, and splitting or combining the CEO and board chairman roles.

The general question is whether there is any association between such company practices and attracting a high density of QSs. Specifically, the focus is on the percentage of companies following (or not following) a given practice that appear high (or low) in the QSDR. For example, no association can be asserted if companies following (or not following) a given practice are evenly distributed across the 2,070 companies in the QSDR; but if the practice group members skew mostly toward the high (say 50 percent are in the top 10 percent) or low end of the pool, such an association can be

Table A.1
Panel of selected data points

Nominal variables	Total sample no.	No. in QSDR	% in QSDR	Within the QSDR (#)			Within the QSDR (%)		
				Top 10%	Top 25%	Top 50%	Top 10%	Top 25%	Top 50%
Branding	38	36	95%	13	27	35	36%	75%	97%
Chair-CEO	245	234	96%	66	132	197	28%	56%	84%
Drucker	150	141	94%	39	76	119	28%	54%	84%
CEO	174	140	80%	37	79	105	26%	56%	75%
Business Roundtable	183	135	74%	34	74	109	25%	55%	81%
Split-chair	229	216	94%	37	92	184	17%	43%	85%
Dual class	225	135	60%	15	41	86	11%	30%	64%
Low pay	26	22	85%	2	6	14	9%	27%	64%

asserted. (No assertions are made about causation based on the data.) Table A.1 summarizes some of the statistics on these relationships that are cited throughout the book in context.

As a caveat, this exercise relates data sets determined using methods that necessarily differ from those used to create the QSDR. For example, the QSDR sample is limited to companies of a minimum size ($1.2 billion market cap), type (e.g., excluding REITs, or Real Estate Investment Trusts), public company history (at least four years), and U.S./Canadian domicile. In contrast, the comparative data are generated in various different ways. As examples:

- those signing the Business Roundtable mission statement include nonpublic companies;
- the dual-class survey consulted was based on the Russell 3000; and
- the compilation of companies paying CEOs nominal salaries is drawn from the entire population of public company filings dating back a decade.

When comparing such data to the QSDR, therefore, only a portion of the former group may appear on the latter list, without implying anything about shareholder quality of those not appearing. On the other hand, the interpretation of the data that are strongly in one direction or another is described more fully in the chapters of this book than in the abbreviated assertions stated above.

Further General Notes

A common pitfall of books on corporate strategy, and some research, is overemphasizing past successes and related practices to extrapolate advice or prescriptions.[5] In general, this involves selecting a dozen or so success stories around a theme, identifying commonalities, and prescribing emulation. Such efforts, well intentioned though they invariably are, overlook causation. The successes may not be caused by the commonalities at all, but may be due to luck or happenstance.

In this book's case, I identify scores of companies boasting a high relative density of QSs, observe commonalities, and suggest other companies adopt some of the commonalities and investors to weigh them. Yet it is possible that some such commonalities had little or nothing to do with the resulting shareholder bases, which instead are greatly influenced by randomness or happenstance. While such a critique may seem farfetched, remaining downside can be further mitigated in a couple of ways.

First, instead of sampling only for success, sample for failure: companies also sharing the commonalities but not getting the shareholders. These certainly exist. The propensity is evident even among the successes, which show a range of results. All those featured in this book, even those in the top quartile, still have substantial indexers and transients. Put a different way, given the prevailing shareholder universe, even those firms doing their level best to attract a substantial cohort of QSs may not be able to do so. (Another countersample would seek companies not sharing the commonalities but getting the shareholders anyway. These certainly exist as well. Examples are technology companies that achieved power and scale in the past decade, such as Facebook. They have also attracted substantial QS bases, though this may be due more to the compelling economics of their franchises than to their exercising any of the levers described in this book.)

Second, the critique ultimately cautions about learning from past successes because so many factors are at work. They operate in a cumulative process where one element is almost certainly luck and the question is the relative roles of strategy versus luck.

This problem can be mitigated by focusing on subjects for which the cumulative processes are richer such that those factors most probably play more of a relative role than luck.

That seems to be the case here, where success requires that multiple elements of philosophy and practice must converge across shareholder engagement, corporate tailoring, and board engagement. But, finally, all these are decided safe practices for corporations with limited risk of adverse side effects. They are also cheap. The prescription is conservatively calculated to do no harm while promising significant improvements.

Netting to Names

Based on the foregoing tabulations and explanations, the following are some integrated lists of individual and institutional QSs and companies that attract them in high density.

Individual QSs		
Chuck Akre	Ingrid Hendershot	Bill Ruane
Andy Brown	Mellody Hobson	Tom Russo
Chris Browne	Irving Kahn	Fayez Sarofim
Warren Buffett	John Maynard Keynes	Walter Schloss
Susan Byrne	Seth Klarman	Sir John Templeton
Shelby Davis	Barbara Marcin	Joel Tillinghast
David Dreman	Bill Miller	Hans Utsch
Phil Fisher	John Neff	Ralph Wanger
Glenn Greenberg	T. Rowe Price	Marty Whitman
Robert Hagstrom	Robert Robotti	Meryl Witmer
Mason Hawkins	Chuck Royce	

QS Firms

AKO Capital	E. S. Barr	Mar Vista
Akre Capital	Eagle Capital	Mass. Financial
Ariel Investments	Fidelity	Matrix Capital
Aristotle Capital	Fiduciary Management	Medley Brown
Artisan Partners	Findlay Park	Mraz Amerine
Atlanta Investment	First Manhattan	Neuberger Berman
Avenir Corp.	First Pacific	Polen Capital
Baillie Gifford & Co.	Franklin Mutual	Ruane Cunniff
Baker Brothers	Gardner, Russo & Gardner	Scopia Capital
Baron Funds	Giverny Capital	Sleep, Zakaria
Barrow Hanley	Fundsmith	Smead Capital
Baupost	Harris Associates (Oakmark)	Southeastern Asset Management
Beck, Mack & Oliver	Hartford Funds	Speece Thorson
Blue Harbour	Hotchkis & Wiley	Sprucegrove
Broad Run	Iridian Asset Management	State Farm Insurance
Brown Brothers Harriman	Jackson National	Stockbridge Partners
Burgundy Capital	Kahn Brothers	T. Rowe Price
Cantillon Capital	Kensico Capital	Temasek Holdings
Capital Research	Klingenstein Fields	Tweedy, Browne
Capital World	Lafayette Investments	W. H. Reaves
Cedar Rock	Lee, Danner & Bass	Wallace Capital
Davis Selected Advisers	London Co. of Virginia	Water Street Capital
DF Dent	Longview Partners	Wedgewood Partners
Diamond Hill	Lourd Capital	Weitz Investment Management
Dodge & Cox	Lyrical Asset Management	Wellington
Douglass Winthrop		

QS Attractors

3M	Abbott Labs	Accenture
Air Products	Alleghany	Alphabet (Google)
Amazon	AMERCO (U-Haul)	American Tower
Anthem	AutoNation	Berkshire
Bristol-Myers Squibb	Brookfield	Cable One
Capital One	CarMax	Churchill Downs
Clorox	Coca-Cola	Constellation Brands
Constellation Software	Credit Acceptance	Crown Holdings
Danaher	Dover	Enstar
Fairfax Financial	Genuine Parts	Graham Holdings (WaPo)
Hormel Foods	Illinois Tool Works	Intel
Johnson & Johnson	Kimberly Clark	Liberty Media
Loews	Markel	Marsh & McLennan
Mastercard	Microsoft	Mohawk Industries
Morningstar	Nestlé	Netflix
NVR	O'Reilly Automotive	PepsiCo
PNC Financial	Post Holdings	Procter & Gamble
Progressive Corporation	Roper Technologies	Seaboard
Sherwin-Williams	Sirius	Texas Instruments
Thermo Fisher	TransDigm	Unilever
United Technologies	Verisign	Walmart
White Mountains Insurance		

Selected Quality Shareholder Statements

ALL THE INVESTORS WHOSE MISSION statements are excerpted in this appendix are QSs, at the top of the statistical measures of long holding periods and high concentration. They vary on both of course, some concentrated throughout their portfolios, others more diversified beyond their core ten or twenty. Some are consistently at the very top of those metrics, while others move up and down within the top band over successive periods.

All boast impressive returns on investment spanning many years. Together, all hold substantial positions in companies discussed in this book. Roughly estimated assets under management span the range of small, medium, and large. A sampling of substantial holdings in both duration and size also appears.

The excerpts are verbatim, mostly from firm websites, letters, or SEC filings, with omitted words not necessarily indicated by ellipses or other punctuation, and some paragraph headings changed for consistency within this book.

As for the selection process, I read the Form ADV, Part 2A, of all funds in the top twenty, along with a smattering of those in the top one hundred, of the top QSs measured by long holding periods and high concentration, as described in appendix A. I also consulted the websites of all such funds, seeking useful and representative descriptions of their approaches to investing and engagement to develop a portrait of the QS mindset.

Some QSs are more public about their views, while others are quite private. Indeed, quite a few QSs have one-page website pages requiring log-in for clients/employees only. Examples of such funds (and key personalities) include Baupost (and Seth Klarman), Cantillon (William von Mueffling), Lone Pine (David Mandel), and Matrix (David Goel).

Yet other distinguished QSs offer only terse descriptions of investment philosophy, not useful in creating a general portrait. For instance, the Gates Foundation publishes a brief generalized description of investment philosophy, noting that investments are managed by unnamed professionals and that Bill and Melinda participate in casting proxy votes in a do-good manner.

LIST OF FIRMS IN APPENDIX B

AKO Capital
Baillie Gifford
Bush O'Donnell Investment Advisors
Capital Research and Management Company
Cedar Rock Capital Partners
Davis Selected Advisers
Fiduciary Management, Inc.
First Manhattan
Fundsmith
Gardner, Russo & Gardner
Lafayette Investments
Lyrical Asset Management

Ruane, Cunniff & Goldfarb
Southeastern Asset Management
Stockbridge Partners
T. Rowe Price

AKO Capital [AUM $15B]

Long Term. Running a business is a long-term affair. Products take years to develop; winning the trust of customers and building scale in new markets can take even longer. We look for corporate cultures that manifest a long-term vision and companies that share our quest for long-term value creation. Such companies understand the importance of cost efficiency but focus on long-term sustainable growth and return on capital.

Return on Capital, Not Quarterly Earnings. Short-term earnings goals are readily achieved by cost cutting, and revenue growth targets can be hit just by an aggressive acquisition campaign. We prefer companies who develop differentiated customer benefits priced for value and those who allocate capital to R&D and advertising. We prize companies that prioritize return on capital, as that creates compounding value, even though media and analysts fixate on quarterly earnings per share. In general, we also like companies that use return on capital to measure performance and influence incentive compensation plans not only at the top but throughout the organization.

Family Ownership. Durable dynastic firms typically avoid excessive leverage and use retained earnings rather than serial equity offerings to grow.[1] Family-owned businesses fail, of course, sometimes through misplaced confidence in the ability of second or third generation managers. But the distinction between family-owned and family-run can be important, and research tends to confirm our hunch that corporate cultures of family-owned businesses align them with the criteria of quality investing.

Discipline. Good managers have the patience and discipline to invest in organic growth and the willpower to resist the temptation of a dash for growth through "transformational" (and often value destructive) acquisitions. Undisciplined acquisition sprees often signal vain managements, which we do not associate with quality companies. Another sign of long-term thinking is a prudent balance sheet and counter-cyclical investment. Exceptional managers minimize borrowing and turn a recession into an advantage.

Tenacity. Good managers have the tenacity to execute on their long-term vision for a business. The history of Rolls-Royce's civil aerospace division illustrates [this]. After privatization in 1987, Rolls-Royce stuck with its hugely expensive development of Trent engines for wide-bodied aircraft. The company's vision, under two successive chief executives throughout the 1990s, sought first to sell more engines and then to generate recurring revenue through selling ongoing service priced based on an engine's hours in operation. While some short-term shareholders criticized the strategy for its costs during implementation, QSs gained enormously from the managerial vision and persistence.

Baillie Gifford [AUM $100B]

We are not passive investors who think that current share prices capture the future prospects of companies. We don't believe that investment decisions can be made on numbers alone, even by supercomputers and complex algorithms. Passive has its place, providing low-cost market access with, on average, better after-fees results than active managers. However, it has little to do with the process of allocating capital to innovative companies—though on that point it has much in common with many active managers.

We are not a typical active manager either: we believe this term has become a one-size-fits-all description which is very unhelpful for investors. It has been hijacked by many fund managers who think it suggests "activity" and simply being different from an index. The reality is that much of this activity has more to do with trying to outsmart other investors than with the creative deployment of capital, and that defining active as being different from an index is to start in the wrong place. This is why most active investors fail to deliver returns that outperform passive investment strategies over the long term. They're not even trying to do the fundamental job of investing.

Some see the collective failure of active management as an argument to embrace passive. We see it as an opportunity to redefine our original purpose of deploying clients' capital into tangible, returns-generating activities. And we believe that redefinition is "actual investment."

We believe our approach to investing not only best delivers good outcomes for clients, but also helps to develop great companies that provide for the needs and wants of people, thereby benefitting society as a whole. Investing responsibly for the long term is not counter to outperforming for clients, it's intrinsic to it.

Bush O'Donnell Investment Advisors [AUM <$1B]

We pursue a low-volatility, long-term investment philosophy for clients who seek to preserve and build assets over time. We invest in a portfolio of companies that have a proven track record of growing earnings at a credible 9 percent to 11 percent per year. The style is concentrated, with investments in 15 to 20 U.S. domiciled large- and mid-capitalization common stocks. We believe this is sufficient constituent diversification to eliminate most of the idiosyncratic risk (risk of over-concentration in a single security) in the portfolio, and serves to impose a strict discipline on portfolio management decisions. [We impose] an individual position maximum of 12 percent. We have a long investment horizon; portfolio turnover is low, averaging 15 percent per year.

Capital Research and Management Company [wholly owned subsidiary of the Capital Group Companies, Inc., AUM $2T]

An investment philosophy that is distinguished by four key beliefs:

- Solid research is fundamental to sound investment decisions. Capital Research and Management Company employs teams of experienced analysts who regularly gather in-depth, first-hand information on markets and companies around the globe.
- Investment decisions should not be made lightly. In addition to providing extensive research, our investment professionals go to great lengths to determine the difference between the fundamental value of a company and its price in the marketplace.
- A long-term approach. It's part of the big-picture view our investment professionals take of the companies in which we invest. This is reflected by the typically low turnover of portfolio holdings in the funds we manage. In addition, our investment professionals usually remain with us for many years and are compensated according to their investment results over time.
- The Capital System. Capital Research and Management Company uses a system of multiple portfolio managers in managing most account and fund assets. Under this approach, the portfolio of a fund or account is divided into segments managed by individual managers who decide how their respective segments will be invested. In addition, Capital Research and Management Company's investment analysts may make investment decisions with respect to a portion of a fund's or client's portfolio. Over time, this method has contributed to consistency of results and continuity of management.

Cedar Rock Capital Partners [AUM $12B]

Our investment approach is to buy and hold shares in companies that we believe capable of compounding in value over the long term. Our investment criteria emphasize quality, value, and managerial character. We define high-quality businesses as being capable of sustaining high returns on their operating capital employed without requiring financial leverage, and of reinvesting at least a portion of their excess cash flows at high rates of return. We consider such companies to be attractively valued when their normalized excess cash flows, calculated as a percentage of the companies' equity market capitalizations, compare favorably with long-term interest rates.

We devote much of our research effort to assessing corporate managers for their probity, trustworthiness and ability to reinvest their corporate cash flows at attractive rates of returns for shareholders. Our criteria are demanding and our portfolios tend to be concentrated in approximately 20 companies, selected globally. We make no effort to minimize volatility relative to any national, regional, or global index of equity market performance. However, we expect our emphasis on both quality and value to generate satisfactory absolute and relative performance over the long term.

Davis Selected Advisers [AUM $40B]

Management. Great businesses are built by first-class management teams. Often these are individuals who think like owner-operators, who consider the strategic and operational implications of their decisions, who allocate capital on a day-to-day basis in a financially productive fashion, and who manage risk in a manner that maximizes shareholder value over full market cycles. We view management as partners and place great value on those individuals who by their actions exhibit an exceptional degree of intelligence, energy, and integrity.

Business. The best long-term investments are typically durable, well-managed businesses that thrive in good times and have the financial strength to weather more challenging environments. We seek to invest in businesses that generate ample free cash flow from products and services that are not prone to obsolescence risk, earn high and/or improving returns on capital, and ideally are well positioned to benefit from long-term secular tailwinds.

Moats. Capital tends to flow to businesses offering the highest returns. Therefore, even the strongest, most well-managed businesses must constantly build and maintain formidable competitive advantages over competitors in order to preserve their superior economics. To maximize our chances of compounding our clients' capital effectively over full market cycles, we have a strong preference for businesses with wide (and growing) competitive moats. The moats may include globally recognized brands, a dominant or growing share in a growing market, a superior profit model, a lean cost structure, unique distribution advantages, unique intellectual property, and so forth.

Fiduciary Management, Inc. [AUM $24B]

We utilize a business owner's approach to investing, thoroughly examining the economics of the business and the quality of the management team.

Our approach is contrarian in nature; we invest in companies that have stumbled or are temporarily out of favor with the market, and hence, improperly priced.

Our goal is to invest in durable business franchises that are selling at a discount to their intrinsic value.

We believe our investment process of purchasing good companies at discount valuations will achieve superior risk-adjusted returns over a full market cycle.

First Manhattan [AUM $25B]

Businesses. We buy businesses for our clients, rather than stocks which represent pieces of paper. We do extensive research on every investment before we decide to make a commitment. Our intended holding period is a very long time; we want to be convinced that these are understandable businesses with strong management, a good long-term record of profitability, and a favorable industry environment that will allow for continued growth.

Quality and Price. As value-oriented, long-term investors, we believe the discipline calls for fundamental research, thorough accounting-oriented financial analysis, and the exercise of sound judgment. We seek to find and invest in undervalued businesses at attractive prices. These companies are often trading at a "discount" to their intrinsic value due to temporary issues that lead to a market overreaction.

Selectivity. We do not aim to replicate the broader market. Instead, we seek to own a select group of companies with proven track records of shareholder value creation. We seek companies that generate strong cash flow, have a responsible level of debt (relative to their industry), and have managements that deploy capital in a shareholder-friendly way.

Hold. We strive to minimize changes in a portfolio in order to limit capital gains taxes for our taxable clients. To that end, we look to invest in companies with strong and understandable underlying businesses, leading competitive positioning, and long runways for future growth. We tend to own these companies for an extended period of time, enabling our clients to reap the benefits of compounding value of their accounts over a long period.

Fundsmith [AUM $18B]

On Costs. Fundsmith does not intend to run a passive or index fund, far from it. But investment activity in the form of buying and selling shares has a frictional cost in terms of the commissions and the difference between the bid-offer spread which dealers charge. The more we can minimise these costs, the better.

On Rivals. A recent study by academics at Yale School of Management, using the Active Share methodology, showed that "active" mutual funds in the US with a low Active Share ("index huggers" or "closet indexers") had about 30 percent of all assets in 2003, compared to almost zero in the 1980s, and that low Active Share funds have poor benchmark adjusted returns and do even worse after expenses.

At Fundsmith we are never going to discuss tracking error. Tracking error is the measure of how closely a portfolio tracks the index against which it is benchmarked. In fact, we embrace tracking error. We want to diverge from the benchmarks. In a positive way, of course. So we don't want our owners to be confused into believing that tracking error is a problem or even a legitimate subject for thought or discussion or to waste any time on it.

Most fund managers own too many stocks. Apart from making their performance track the indices, which you can achieve much more cheaply with an index fund, this also makes it difficult for them to invest in the companies they own with conviction. How much can you know about the 80th company in your portfolio?

Most fund management groups also manage a proliferation of funds. We could be forgiven for thinking that the strategy of many fund management groups is to raise a new fund for every possible investment technique and for every new fad and to hope that at least some of them succeed in a random process and that you don't notice the ones which don't.

You may notice that our fund's name is simple: the Fundsmith Equity Fund. It doesn't say it's a Growth Fund or an Income Fund. Our marketing advisers were very keen for us to get the word Income or Dividend into the title because apparently income funds outsell growth funds. We haven't followed that advice because we regard the distinction between income and growth as artificial.

Buy and Hold. We aim to be long-term, buy-and-hold investors. We seek to own only stocks that will compound in value over the years. Accordingly, we have to be very careful about the stocks we pick. We believe, as does Warren Buffett, that we do not have a good investment idea every day, or indeed, not even every year. Consequently, we should treat our investment career like one of those tickets you get for a tram which is spent once it's been punched 20 times, as that's the number of great investment ideas we're likely to be able to find at a price we can justify investing in them. This also minimises the frictional cost of trading.

Quality Businesses. A high quality business is one which can sustain a high return on operating capital employed. In cash. It's funny how investors who are not at all confused about this concept when they are seeking the bank deposit with the highest rate of interest (necessarily balanced by risk, as depositors in Icelandic banks discovered) or even the return on a fund such as ours, lose their marbles when it comes to evaluating companies. They start talking about growth in earnings per share and other gibberish. Earnings per share is not the same as cash, but more importantly it takes no account of the capital employed to generate those earnings or the return which is earned on it.

Conservative Leverage. We only invest in companies that earn a high return on their capital on an unleveraged basis. The companies may well have leverage, but they don't require borrowed money to function.

Resilient Businesses. An important contributor to resilience is a resistance to product obsolescence. This means that we do not invest in industries which are subject to rapid technological innovation.

Benchmark Skepticism. Over a sufficient period of time, you will no doubt want to assess our performance against a range of benchmarks—the performance of cash, bonds, equities, and other funds, and we will assist you in that process by providing comparisons. However, we do not think it is helpful to make comparisons with movements in other asset prices or indices over the short term, as we are not trying to provide short term performance. Be warned: in our view, even a year is a short period to measure things by. Moreover, a year does not have its foundations in the business or investment cycle. It is, in fact, the time it takes the earth to go around the sun and is therefore of more use in studying astronomy than investment.

Conservative Diversification. We do seek portfolio diversification, but the strictness of our investment criteria will inevitably leave us with a concentrated portfolio of 20–30 companies. We do not fear the concentration risk which this brings for two reasons. We do not fear the concentration risk which this brings [as] research has shown that you can achieve close to optimal diversity with 20 stocks.

Management Versus Numbers. We are rather more comfortable analyzing numbers than we are trying to gain insights into companies by meeting the management. We intend to find companies which are potential investments by a screening process of their financial results to identify high return, cash generative, consistently performing businesses.

That is not to say that we don't meet management. It is important to assess whether management provides honest stewardship, acting in the interests of the owners and telling it how it is rather than PR spin to try to enhance investors' perceptions. This does not mean we seek management with a narrow focus on what has become labelled "shareholder value." Too often a reliance upon the simplistic targets required by shareholder activists, such as growth in earnings per share and returning capital to make the balance sheet "efficient," (sometimes so efficient that it busts the company) has been to the long term detriment of shareholders.

It's important to remember we are a minority investor in large quoted companies rather than a private equity investor with a controlling stake in a company who can control management. We do engage with management in an effort to ensure that their decisions are in the long term interests of the company and in particular in relation to capital allocation and management remuneration which we regard as vital. But ultimately, our main sanction in the event that management is behaving badly or illogically is to not own the shares.

Gardner, Russo & Gardner [AUM $15B]

Method. We conduct research by analyzing a company's financial reports, attending annual, industry, and analyst meetings, and engaging its management in appropriate venues. We assess its free-cash-flow generation, sustainability of franchise, earnings and pricing power, and quality of management.

Buy and Hold. We hope to hold positions for many years. Our focused familiarity with each of our holdings gives us the confidence to do this, and allows us to pass on to our clients the advantages of low turnover such as minimized taxes and transaction costs. Long holding periods promote in our investors the mindset of business owners; this properly focuses attention away from the short-term noise that can distract from long-term value creation.

Commitment. The largest positions can have weighting in the high single- to low double-digits as a percentage of the portfolio. We believe this method of portfolio construction offers a reasonable amount of diversification while concentrating funds in the best investment ideas that our highly focused research efforts uncover.

Moats. To merit our investing attention a company must possess unique characteristics. Its businesses' competitive advantages must give indication of stability and growth. This is measured by its sustainable long-term returns on capital and by consistent generation of free cash flow. The company must be run by a management team with a proven record of successful operation and effective allocation of free cash flow.

Owner Culture. It must also possess the type of firm culture that provides the context and incentive for long-term value creation. This means a management that brings the most effective of "family-owned" approaches to running their operations (long-term wealth-building rather than short-term profit-harvesting; interest in proactively maintaining reputational value of a business; deep knowledge of its businesses and of the industry in which its businesses operate).

Strength. We look to invest in companies which have the "capacity to reinvest" that are run by shareholder-minded managements who have the "capacity to suffer" Wall Street disapproval while directing heavy investments intended to generate future growth but which all-too-often adversely impact near-term reported profits.

Focus. [Portfolio concentration] may mean temporary depression of market values for companies if and when they are out of favor. However, reduced share prices as a result of market sentiment do not necessarily relate to reduced prospects for our companies' operations. Accordingly, we prefer not to move from sector to sector, following the bubble of the moment. Rather, we prefer to patiently await the market's return to recognition of our businesses' intrinsic value.

Nonetheless, this may mean that our portfolios undergo periodic under-performance versus the market as a whole. The same can be said for individual companies in which we invest. Earnings may disappoint without necessarily indicating any decrease in our long-term confidence for a company's ability to grow intrinsic value. Because our core positions can be heavily weighted, performance of our portfolios can be dampened by market sentiment, which we regard, however, as immaterial to our investments' long-term potential.

Long-Term. As patient investors, we await the market's recognition of the intrinsic value of our portfolio companies' shares. In fact, the deeper the discount our shares enjoy from their intrinsic value, the more unrealized wealth we build within a portfolio. The freedom to ignore consensus and with it quarterly and annual targets is critical to our long-term outlook.

Lafayette Investments [AUM <$1B]

We live in an era of shareholder activists. To counter this movement, it seems logical that corporations should seek to attract long-term knowledgeable shareholders who support management's vision. The question is how to do so. Since any reasonably competent CEO knows what investors like ourselves want to hear, investors need to go a step further and look for tangible evidence of pro-shareholder behavior. We suggest the following to attract the right type of shareholder:

(1) write a candid shareholder letter, (2) have a compensation system with proper incentives that is simple enough to fit in a few pages of the proxy statement, (3) do away with earnings guidance, (4) keep stock options to a minimum, (5) only buy back shares when they are cheap, (6) conduct shareholder-friendly annual meetings, (7) if you must hold a quarterly conference call, be as forthright as possible with difficult issues, (8) do away with adjusted earnings, (9) see evidence of open market purchases of stock by insiders, (10) present a long-term vision and provide yearly updates, and (11) have a clear vision of capital allocation priorities.

Any company that has a sound business and shows evidence of complying with most of these objectives is almost certain to attract shareholders like ourselves.

Lyrical Asset Management [AUM $7B]

We are fundamental value investors. The combination of value investing with quality and analyzability distinguishes the Lyrical investment program. . . . While attractive valuation is the most important thing, it is not the only thing we require in an investment. We will only invest in quality companies. We seek businesses that we believe will generate attractive returns on their invested capital. We seek resilient businesses, those with reasonable debt levels, positive growth, attractive margins, competent management, and the flexibility to react to all phases of the business cycle. Our quality discipline leads us to avoid deeply cyclical companies, basic materials and commodities, and regulated utilities.

We will only invest in companies we can thoroughly analyze and understand. Certain businesses do not lend themselves to fundamental analysis, either because of complexity or opacity. Examples include banks, pharmaceuticals, biotech, and high tech. We avoid such businesses by design. We believe that the better one can analyze a company, the more likely one is to be right.

Ruane, Cunniff & Goldfarb [AUM $25B]

We have been investing for the long term for nearly 50 years, across multiple market cycles, portfolio managers, and generations of leadership. The way we execute our strategy has evolved over the years, but the basic principles of value investing that guide our judgments have never changed and never will.

Quality. We own quality businesses run by quality people that can compound their earnings rapidly. We hold these businesses over a long horizon with the mindset of a long-term business owner. We buy them for less than what a conservative business person would pay for them. We focus on our best ideas, while avoiding excessive concentration.

Long Term. We think investing with an unusually long-term perspective moves us from the realm of the unpredictable to the realm of the understandable.

Business Owners. We don't believe in target prices. We know that value exists within a range, and is hard for even a thoughtful analyst to pinpoint. We are also sensitive to reinvestment risk. Great companies at good prices are hard to find. If we sold them every time they reached fair value, we could struggle to find replacements. Then there is expense risk. Trading and taxes create real costs with real consequences, even if they're not immediately apparent in headline returns. Our long-term view means that business results, rather than value arbitrage, drive our returns. As such, we have a low inclination to trade.

Know What We Own. Reading company filings and crunching numbers is just the start of our research process. We take pride and pleasure in investigating a company from all angles, doing the kind of on-the-ground, primary research that an enterprising journalist might do. This sort of intensive primary research is how we spend most of our time.

We're Picky. We prize the outliers—the companies that define a market or dominate a niche; companies that are far superior to the average business. Most of the time, wonderful businesses trade expensively in the stock market. We try to wait for and capitalize on the rare moments when they can be purchased for a discount to their intrinsic values that incorporates what we consider the single most important concept in investing: a margin of safety. Our small collection of investments bears little resemblance to the S&P 500 or any other index. In fact, our top ten investments often account for >60 percent of the value of our portfolios. The S&P 500 may be relevant for assessing our performance over the long term, but it has no bearing on how we construct our portfolios.

Southeastern Asset Management [AUM $45B]

Quality. We invest in strong businesses that are understandable, financially sound, competitively positioned, and have ample free cash flow that may grow over time. These businesses are run by good people—honorable and trustworthy, highly skilled operators and capital allocators, who are focused on building value per share and have incentives aligned with their shareholders.

Long-Term. We seek to take advantage of short-term market emotions. We are long-term owners, not traders or speculators, and invest for the long-term based on objective intrinsic values with a horizon of at least five years.

Concentration. We construct our portfolios with what we believe to be our best 18–22 global investment ideas. Concentrating allows for adequate diversification while providing some of the best opportunities to maximize returns and minimize loss of principal.

Partnership. Our investment team views our portfolio company management teams and boards of directors as partners, and we engage with them to ensure the greatest value for shareholders over the long term.

Stockbridge Partners [unit of Berkshire Partners, AUM $2.5B]

We take positions in public securities with a bias toward being long-term investors, focusing on high quality companies that exhibit earnings sustainability and growth. We accept short-term volatility—and in many cases, view price fluctuations more as opportunities than as risks.

Long-Term. First, and perhaps most important, we embrace a long-term investment focus. We are explicit on this point: we are patient capital, willing to wait for our investments to prove themselves and not necessarily discouraged by a temporarily out-of-favor enterprise.

Concentrated. Second, we apply this long-term perspective to a concentrated portfolio as we would rather have our portfolio comprised of our best ideas. A company makes its way into our portfolio only after it has been deeply researched and it presents a compelling long-term return.

Engaged. Third, we employ a methodology of deep research, close monitoring, and an active dialogue with management.

T. Rowe Price [AUM $1T]

[Some investors have issued formal statements of their philosophies on shareholder activism. Here is an example from T. Rowe Price.] We are long-term investors. We take a very long-term perspective because well-functioning capital markets and plentiful high-quality investment opportunities are essential to the future of our investment process, our clients, and our firm. Our philosophy on shareholder activism is based on our own observations as experienced, fundamentally oriented investors. The core tenets of our philosophy are:

- We believe each activism campaign represents a unique set of conditions that have combined to create an inflection point for the company involved. We have a responsibility as engaged, active investors to assess each situation on its own merits.
- We believe management teams of companies have better information about their businesses than outside parties do. Therefore, a certain amount of deference is owed to management's assessment of the company's opportunity set.
- Our disciplined, active approach to investment is rooted in our ability to identify, support, and invest in companies

that create sustainable value over time. Neither companies nor activists have cornered the market on great ideas that could generate value. Therefore, we believe company managements and their boards should exhibit openness, curiosity, and intellectual honesty with regard to serious, well-supported ideas for value creation, even when such ideas originate outside the company.

• The time frame we apply for decision-making in activist campaigns is a multiyear view. Our objective is to determine which path is likely to foster sustainable, long-term performance by the company.

The only criteria we use in determining the best course of action in activism campaigns are those related to the long-term interests of our advisory clients. We arrive at voting decisions in contested elections independently. We do not retain outside parties to engage with companies for us. We do not allow the business interests of our firm (for example, client-facing associates) to take part in any discussion or decision-making related to activism campaigns. Although we are clients of ISS for proxy-related research, we do not follow the recommendations of proxy advisors on proxy contests.

Acknowledgments

THANKS TO THE ECOSYSTEM OF QSs for a lifetime of inspiration and support, especially the dean of this group, Warren E. Buffett, for his support of many of my articles and books over more than two decades. In this crowd are hundreds of friends and colleagues who have helped develop and act on the ideas in this book.

For comments on all or parts of drafts of the manuscript, thanks to an impressive roster of quality shareholders, as well as other astute readers: Jonathan Boyar, Patrick Brennan, Randy Cepuch, Torkell Eide, Nicholas Georgakopoulos, Ingrid Hendershot, Mark Hughes, Amanda Katten, Steve Keating, Mark Hughes, Andrew Marks, Howard Marks, Alan Morrison, David Mraz, Phil Ordway, Will Pan, Steve Ross, Andrew Ryasakoff, Myles Thompson, and three anonymous peer reviewers engaged by Columbia University Press.

For insights from outstanding managers, thanks to Joe Brandon (Alleghany), Doug Busk (Credit Acceptance), Charles Fabrikant (SEACOR), Tom Gayner (Markel), Don Graham (WaPo and Graham Holdings), Rich Handler (Jefferies), Weston Hicks (Alleghany), Robert Keane (Cimpress), Bill Lenahan (Four Corners

Property Trust), Mark Leonard (Constellation Software), Kevin O'Donnell (RenRe), Brett Roberts (Credit Acceptance), Joe Steinberg (Leucadia), and Prem Watsa (Fairfax Financial).

For help gathering and analyzing data, thanks to David Templeton of George Washington University, Amanda Kattan (using S&P Capital IQ), Christopher Friend (Floatspec), Martjin Cremers of University of Notre Dame and Ankur Pareek of the University of Nevada, Randall Thomas of Vanderbilt University, Paul Borochin of the University of Connecticut, Rocket Data Systems Inc., and AbdAllah Abualreesh of George Washington University.

Thanks for other vital assistance, from administrative to research, to Annie Ezekilova, my outstanding executive assistant at George Washington University; Gia Arney and Lori Fossum, tenacious research librarians at GW; and Steven Little and his diligent team in GW's Copy Center.

For financial support, especially for a sabbatical research leave, thanks to GW. For physical space and resources, thanks to the libraries of New York University, the Players Club of New York, and the Cosmos Club of Washington, D.C., where I wrote substantial portions of the manuscript.

Above all, for everything under the sun and the moon and beyond, thanks to Stephanie Cuba, my wife of infinite excellence. She is my best editor, best friend, love of my life, and secret sauce. She weighed every word—through multiple drafts—with cheerful tact and wise illumination. Thanks to our two darling daughters, Becca and Sarah, who are an endless inspiration and source of sustenance. This family has my undying gratitude for their deep and abiding support while I spent three years on this project. You are my rock stars and this book is for you.

L. A. C.

Amagansett, New York

May 2020

Notes

Prologue: The Shareholders Managers Deserve

1. See Alon Brav, Wei Jiang, and Tao Li, "Picking Friends Before Picking (Proxy) Fights: How Mutual Fund Voting Shapes Proxy Contests" (Columbia Business School Research Paper 18-16), https://papers.ssrn.com/sol3/papers .cfm?abstract_id=3101473.

2. See Tom C. W. Lin, "Artificial Intelligence, Finance, and the Law," *Fordham Law Review* 88, no. 2 (2019): 531–51.

3. In 2008, Buffett bet a hedge fund manager the S&P 500 would, over the ensuing ten years, outperform, after fees, any hedge fund portfolio the manager cared to assemble. The manager assembled a fund of funds, a configuration charging multiple layers of high fees. During the first three years, the S&P lagged the fund, but by bet's end, the S&P won. If many took from the bet the lesson that indexers are always superior to non-indexed investing, that is a mistake. The primary point was to stress that ordinary individuals are almost certainly better off, given the risks and fees, of staking their savings in index funds rather than entrusting them to high-cost hedge funds.

4. See Martijn Cremers, Jon Fulkerson, and Timothy B. Riley, "Challenging the Conventional Wisdom on Active Management: A Review of the Past 20 Years of Academic Literature on Actively Managed Mutual Funds," *Financial Analysts Journal* 75, no. 4 (2019): 8–35.

5. For some of my discussions of global variation in corporate life, see Lawrence A. Cunningham, "The SEC's Global Accounting Vision: A Realistic Appraisal of a Quixotic Quest," *North Carolina Law Review* 87, no. 1 (2008): 42ff.; Lawrence A. Cunningham, "Commonalities and Prescriptions in the Vertical Dimension of Global Corporate Governance," *Cornell Law Review* 84, no. 5 (1999): 1133–94.

6. See Giovanni Strampelli, "Are Passive Index Funds Active Owners? Corporate Governance Consequences of Passive Investing," *San Diego Law Review* 55, no. 4 (2018): 803–52.

7. See James Woolery, Rob Leclerc, and Richard Fields, "The Ashland-Cruiser Proxy Contest—A Case Study," *Harvard Governance* (blog), February 20, 2019, https://corpgov.law.harvard.edu/2019/02/20/the-ashland-cruiser-proxy -contest-a-case-study.

8. The conscious attraction of QSs is an uncommon practice, and the related literature is limited. Writings on investor relations have long prescribed engaging all shareholders, without regard to attributes or fit. Under this approach, the goal is often to boost the company's stock price. In contrast, the quest of quality investor relations is to promote a rational stock price using a tailored campaign.

In the book *Running an Effective Investor Relations Department: A Comprehensive Guide* (Hoboken, NJ: Wiley, 2012), author Steven Bragg declares dozens of times in the opening chapters that the sole and ultimate goal of investor relations is boosting stock prices. Or consider the subtitle of another broad-gauge book, *Winning Investors Over: Surprising Truths About Honesty, Earnings Guidance, and Other Ways to Boost Your Stock Price* (Brighton, MA: Harvard Business Review Press, 2012) by business school professor Baruch Lev. The subtitle's pitch is striking considering that much of Professor Lev's analysis focuses on business substance, not market price maximization.

Widespread use of the phrase "you get the shareholders you deserve" makes it surprising how little writing addresses what the phrase means or how a company can attract shareholders that complement its business model or culture. Accounting professor Brian Bushee contributed several articles on segmentation of the investment community by characteristic behavior ranging from "transient" to "dedicated"—matching up with Buffett's delineation.

Law professors Edward Rock and Tamara Belinfanti separately reviewed selected levers to shape the shareholder base—both drawing heavily on Buffett. Edward B. Rock, "Shareholder Eugenics in the Public Corporation," *Cornell Law Review* 97, no. 4 (2012): 849–906; Tamara C. Belinfanti, "Shareholder Cultivation and New Governance," *Delaware Journal of Corporation Law* 38 (2014): 789–872.

There is a vast literature on so-called clientele effects, referring to offerings designed to segment a market, and self-selection, referring to autonomous decisions by some in a group to follow one path rather than another. The richest and oldest vein of the clientele effect literature addresses dividend and buyback policy. Yet this literature is often inconclusive and is certainly not comprehensive.

Current conditions in shareholder demographics entice fresh analysis of increasing shareholder fragmentation and what corporations can do about it. This book is intended to spark a rethinking that is long overdue. It does not seem too late, though advances in technology, including artificial intelligence, bode unpredictable change.

1. Meet the Quality Shareholders

1. John F. Wasik, *Keynes's Way to Wealth: Timeless Investment Principles from the Great Economist* (New York: McGraw Hill, 2014).

2. David Chambers, Elroy Dimson, and Justin Foo, "Keynes the Stock Market Investor: A Quantitative Analysis," *Journal of Financial and Quantitative Analysis* 50, no. 4 (2015): 431–49.

3. See Allen C. Benello, Michael Van Biema, and Tobias E. Carlisle, *Concentrated Investing* (Hoboken, N.J.: Wiley, 2016), 48, 51, citing for both points the article by Jason Zweig, "Keynes: One Mean Money Manager," *Wall St. Journal*, April 2, 2012, https://www.wsj.com/articles/SB10001424052702304177104577313810084976558.

4. See Benello, Van Biema, and Carlisle, *Concentrated Investing*, 58.

5. See Lawrence A. Cunningham, *Berkshire Beyond Buffett* (New York: Columbia University Press, 2014).

6. See Benello, Van Biema, and Carlisle, *Concentrated Investing*, 13.

7. Board of Governors of the Federal Reserve System, "Financial Accounts of the United States: Historical Annual Tables (1965–1974)," https://www.federalreserve.gov/releases/z1/20160609/annuals/a1965-1974.pdf.

8. Board of Governors of the Federal Reserve System, "Financial Accounts of the United States: Historical Annual Tables (2005–2015)," at 123, https://www.federalreserve.gov/releases/z1/20160609/annuals/a2005-2015.pdf; Board of Governors of the Federal Reserve System, "Financial Accounts of the United States, Second Quarter 2018," at 130, https://www.federalreserve.gov/releases/z1/20180920/z1.pdf.

9. Anne M. Tucker, "The Long and the Short: Portfolio Turnover Ratios & Mutual Fund Investment Time Horizons," *Iowa Journal of Corporation Law* 43, no. 3 (2018): 581–648.

10. K. J. Martijn Cremers and Simone M. Sepe, "Institutional Investors, Corporate Governance, and Firm Value," *Seattle University Law Review* 41, no. 2 at n. 42 (2018): 387–418.

11. See Tom C. W. Lin, "Artificial Intelligence, Finance, and the Law," *Fordham Law Review* 88, no. 2 (2019): 531–51.

12. See Lawrence A. Cunningham and Stephanie Cuba, "Annual Shareholder Meetings: From Populist to Virtual," *Financial History* (Fall 2018): 14–19.

13. See J. Coffee, L. Lowenstein, and S. Rose-Ackerman, eds., *Knights, Raiders and Targets* (New York: Oxford University Press, 1988).

14. See William W. Bratton and Joseph A. McCahery, eds., introduction to *Institutional Investor Activism: Hedge Funds and Private Equity, Economics and Regulation* (New York: Oxford University Press, 2015), 1–38.

15. See Jennifer L. Blouin, Brian J. Bushee, and Stephanie A. Sikes, "Measuring Tax-Sensitive Institutional Investor Ownership," *Accounting Review* 19, no. 6 (2017): 49–76.

16. See Ashwini K. Agrawal, "Corporate Governance Objectives of Labor Union Shareholders: Evidence from Proxy Voting," *Review of Financial Studies* 25, no. 1 (2012): 187–226.

17. See David Webber, *The Rise of the Working-Class Shareholder: Labor's Last Best Weapon* (Cambridge: Harvard University Press, 2018).

18. Professor Bushee collated his research articles on this subject in a retrospective piece, Brian Bushee, "Identifying and Attracting the 'Right' Investors," *Journal of Applied Corporate Finance* 16, no. 4 (2004): 28–35.

19. For a more extended discussion of research based on Bushee's work, see Lawrence A. Cunningham, "The Case for Empowering Quality Share-holders," *Brigham Young University Law Review* (2020), https://papers.ssrn.com/sol3/papers.cfm?abstract_id=3547482].

20. Some research suggests that biological and sociological factors influence an investor's philosophy and approach, including as between "value investors" and "growth investors." See Henrik Cronqvista, Stephan Siegel, and Frank Yua, "Value Versus Growth Investing: Why Do Different Investors Have Different Styles?," *Journal of Financial Economics* 117, no. 2 (2015): 333–49.

21. From the Ruane Cunniff website statement, https://www.ruanecunniff.com/Philosophy.

22. Draws on Baillie Gifford website statement.

23. Steve Strongin, Robert D. Boroujerdi, Amanda Hindlian, Sandra Lawson, Sonya Banerjee, and Katherine Maxwell, *Directors' Dilemma: Responding to the Rise of Passive Investing*, Goldman Sachs Global Markets Institute (2017), https://www.goldmansachs.com/insights/public-policy/directors-dilemma-f/report.pdf.

24. From the Baillie Gifford website, https://www.bailliegifford.com.

25. See, for example, T. Rowe Price's Investment Philosophy on Shareholder Activism (July 2018), https://www.troweprice.com/content/dam/trowecorp/Pdfs/Shareholder_Activism.pdf.

26. Appendix A describes the research and method for determining rankings based on these characteristics.

27. Families of benchmarks propagate multiple indexes, now aggregating as many as sixty across multiple different brands. These include Dow Jones (at least six: DJ Industrial Average, DJ US Select Dividend, DJ Wilshire 4500, and DJ Wilshire 5000); FTSE (four: FTSE High Dividend Yield, FTSE RAFI US 100, and Mid Small 1500); NASDAQ (two: NASDAQ 100 and the NASDAQ Composite); and Schwab (two, including the Schwab 1000 and Schwab Small Cap). Dozens more are offered by several behemoths, delineating among small, mid, and large cap plus their value and growth components: MSCI (fifteen different ones), S&P (fourteen), and Russell (thirteen).

28. See Tucker, "The Long and The Short."

29. For example, in the period immediately before the global pandemic that began in March 2020, the total market cap of the Russell 3000 was about $30 trillion. Of that, operators of the largest passive indexers commanded nearly half at around $14 trillion (though some run stock-picking funds too). As a group, pension funds (which are much prone to quasi-indexing, though some to dedication) held about one-third or $9 trillion. Activist hedge funds own a sliver—around $100 billion or 1 percent—though they back that capital with powerful game-changing strategies for companies. Given the high level of aggregate share turnover—average holding periods barely near one year—many on the typical shareholder list don't stay a long time, making for a sizable portion of transients.

More specifically, five of the largest activist hedge funds command in aggregate perhaps $100 billion (Carl Ichan, Third Point, ValueAct, Pershing, and Trian), whereas the largest four financial institutions manage $14 trillion (BlackRock, State Street, Vanguard, Fidelity). Among pension funds, the five largest together run nearly $1 trillion (CalPERs, CALSTRs, STRS Ohio). The quality-investing cohort represents the rest. Yet the power of even such relatively small stakes is immense. For perspective, the largest listed companies now boast market caps around $1 trillion, and many smaller ones around $4 to $10 billion.

30. See Eugene F. Fama and Kenneth R. French, "Value Versus Growth: The International Evidence," *Journal of Finance* 53, no. 6 (2002): 1975–99 (worldwide from 1975–1995, "value stocks" outperformed "growth stocks" by 7.68 percent annually).

31. See Martijn Cremers, Jon Fulkerson, and Timothy B. Riley, "Challenging the Conventional Wisdom on Active Management: A Review of the

Past 20 Years of Academic Literature on Actively Managed Mutual Funds," *Financial Analysts Journal* 75, no. 4 (2019): 1–28.

32. Mark Carhart, "On Persistence in Mutual Fund Performance," *Journal of Finance* 52, no. 1 (1997): 57–82 (finding that the empirical evidence did "not support the existence of skilled or informed mutual fund portfolio managers"). Michael Jensen conducted an earlier kindred study. Michael Jensen, "The Performance of Mutual Funds in the Period 1945–1964," *Journal of Finance* 23, no. 2 (1967): 389–416.

33. William Sharpe, "The Arithmetic of Active Management," *Financial Analysts Journal* 47, no. 1 (1991): 7–9.

34. Carhart, "On Persistence in Mutual Fund Performance."

35. Eugene Fama and Kenneth French, "Luck Versus Skill in the Cross-Section of Mutual Fund Performance," *Journal of Finance* 65, no. 5 (2010): 1915–47.

36. Jonathan Berk and Jules van Binsbergen, "Measuring Skill in the Mutual Fund Industry," *Journal of Financial Economics* 118, no. 1 (2015): 1–20; Jonathan B. Berk and Jules H. van Binsbergen, "Mutual Funds in Equilibrium," *Annual Review of Financial Economics* 9 (2017): 147–67; Hyunglae Jeon, Jangkoo Kang, and Changjun Lee, "Precision About Manager Skill, Mutual Fund Flows, and Performance Persistence," *North American Journal of Economics and Finance* 40 (2017): 222–37.

37. Nicolas Bollen and Jeffrey Busse, "Short-Term Persistence in Mutual Fund Performance," *Review of Financial Studies* 19, no. 2 (2005): 569–97; Robert Kowoski, Allan Timmermann, Russ Wermers, and Hal White, "Can Mutual Fund 'Stars' Really Pick Stocks? New Evidence from a Bootstrap Analysis," *Journal of Finance* 61, no. 6 (2006): 2551–96.

38. Yakov Amihud and Ruslan Goyenko, "Mutual Fund's R2 as Predictor of Performance," *Review of Financial Studies* 26, no. 3 (2013): 667–94; Martijn Cremers and Antti Petajisto, "How Active Is Your Fund Manager? A New Measure That Predicts Performance," *Review of Financial Studies* 22, no. 9 (2009): 3329–65.

39. Martijn Cremers, "Active Share and the Three Pillars of Active Management: Skill, Conviction, and Opportunity," *Financial Analysts Journal* 73, no. 2 (2017): 61–79.

40. Larry Swedroe, "Active Share: Does It Predict Fund Performance?," *Alpha Architect* (blog), June 15, 2017, https://alphaarchitect.com/2017/06/15/active-share-predict-fund-performance.

41. Wesley Gray, "Is Passive Perfect? High Active Share Long-Term Investing Works Better," *Alpha Architect* (blog), April 30, 2015, https://alphaarchitect.com/2015/04/30/is-passive-perfect-high-active-share-long-term-investing-works-better.

42. See Jeremy J. Siegel, *Stocks for the Long Run*, 5th ed. (New York: McGraw-Hill Education, 2014); see also Louis Engel and Henry R. Hecht, *How to Buy Stocks*, 8th ed. (New York: Little, Brown, 1994).

43. See Burton G. Malkiel, *A Random Walk Down Wall Street*, 12th ed. (New York: Norton, 2019).

44. Howard Marks, "Investing Without People" (2018 letter to Oaktree Capital shareholders). Marks's earlier letters were compiled into his 2011 book, *The Most Important Thing* (New York: Columbia University Press, 2011).

45. See Boyar Research, "Boyar's Index Orphans," 43, nos. 7/8, October 12, 2017. http://genderi.org/pars_docs/refs/68/67567/67567.pdf.

46. Some readers will be interested in a bit more color on this aspect of the debate. Pioneering research began in 2009 with Martijn Cremers and Antti Petajisto, who have periodically refined their work. They developed a measure of active fund management: a portfolio's uniqueness versus a fund's own benchmark, called active share, reflecting the degree to which a fund's portfolio differs from its benchmark index portfolio. See Martijn Cremers and Antti Petajisto, "How Active Is Your Fund Manager? A New Measure that Predicts Performance," *Review of Financial Studies* 22, no. 9 (2009): 3329–65; see also Antti Petajisto, "Active Share and Mutual Fund Performance," *Financial Analysts Journal* 69, no. 4 (2013): 73–93 (updating and extending the study).

Acknowledging that active funds in aggregate may underperform market indexes, they found that higher active share funds are more likely to outperform their benchmarks, while lower active share funds are less likely to outperform their benchmarks. They proposed adding this as a data point for customers and others to evaluate portfolio managers. In some ways, the assertion is unremarkable. After all, it is a truism that to outperform an index, a portfolio must differ from that index. To outperform, however, requires differences that add value, so a randomly selected portfolio of stocks is unlikely to outperform. As a result, the conclusions took on a life of their own.

The work drew considerable attention in the investment community and mainstream media. Funds with high active shares touted this trait in marketing materials, while customers shopped around accordingly. Such interest, amplified by news stories, inspired many critical research reviews, including several rival studies by researchers at leading indexers, including BlackRock, Vanguard, and AQR.

Using a different data set, the Vanguard researchers reported finding that higher active shares did not predict outperformance. In addition, they found that higher active share funds were both costlier and riskier—fees were higher and returns more dispersed. See Todd Schlanger, Christopher B. Philips, and Karin Peterson LaBarge, "The Search for Outperformance: Evaluating

'Active Share,' " *Vanguard Investment Perspectives* 12 (2012). That said, the Vanguard researchers acknowledged that active share could be useful as part of an overall evaluation of portfolio management.

Similarly, the BlackRock researchers found that active share alone could make outperformance less likely, rejecting the assertion that conviction alone mattered. Ananth Madhavan, Aleksander Sobczyk, and Andrew Ang, "Estimating Time-Varying Factor Exposures with Cross-Sectional Characteristics with Application to Active Mutual Fund Returns," *Financial Analysts Journal* 73, no. 4 (2017): 41–54. While acknowledging that skillful stock pickers may exist, they concluded that conviction proxied by active share is insufficient to identify the cohort upfront.

Finally, the AQR team called the empirical evidence "weak" and attributable entirely to a correlation between active share and the corresponding benchmark type. Andrea Frazzini, Jacques Friedman, and Lukasz Pomorski, "Deactivating Active Share," *Financial Analysts Journal* 72, no. 2 (2016): 14–21. After all, high and low active share funds have different benchmarks. Most high active share funds are small cap, while most low active share funds are large cap. Conclusion: active share does not predict returns.

The AQR paper drew impassioned responses from the active share developers. Professor Petajisto posted a five-page rebuttal to the fourteen-page article, opening by declaiming that "all of the key claims of AQR's paper were already addressed" in the original scholarship. After delineating those claims and earlier discussions, Petajisto concluded: "Ignoring large and essential parts" of the subject articles is "simply not the way to conduct impartial scientific inquiry."

Professor Cremers wrote an entire paper in response, arguing that the AQR paper "should not be interpreted using typical academic standards." Martijn Cremers, "AQR in Wonderland: Down the Rabbit Hole of 'Deactivating Active Share' (and Back Out Again?)," *SSRN*, June 30, 2015, papers .ssrn.com.abstract_id=2625214. He asserted that undisclosed information in the AQR team's data contradicted their critical conclusions, and in any event, AQR, a fund complex itself, has a very low active share score. Moreover, accepting the point that benchmark styles matter, Cremers stood by the robustness of his earlier conclusions. In particular, in the modest mode first reported, active share "is only one tool among many to analyze investment funds" and may "plausibly help investors improve their returns."

Impartial observers of this research food fight recognized value and legitimate points on both sides. Cremers and Petajisto are certainly right that active share is a useful measure of portfolio concentration. They also drew praise for showing that conviction is a prerequisite to outperformance— and especially for funds charging high fees for delivering mostly an index.

See Martijn Cremers and Quinn Curtis, "Do Mutual Fund Investors Get What They Pay For? The Legal Consequences of Closet Index Funds," *Virginia Law & Business Review* 11, no. 1 (2017): 31–94. On the other hand, concentration alone is insufficient to deliver sustained predictable outsized returns. A strategy is required.

2. Comparative Advantages

1. See Jennifer Riel and Roger Martin, "How Unilever Won Over Shareholders with Its Long-Term Approach," *Globe & Mail*, October 13, 2017.
2. Many such Unilever shareholders were index funds, but Unilever also attracted some venerable QSs, such as AKO Capital, Gardner, Russo & Gardner, and Hotchkis & Wiley.
3. Yair Listokin, "Management Always Wins the Close Ones," *American Law and Economics Review* 10, no. 2 (2008): 159–84.
4. See Laurent Bach and Daniel Metzger, "How Close Are Close Shareholder Votes?," *Review of Financial Studies* 32, no. 8 (2019): 3183–214.
5. Jill E. Fisch, Assaf Hamdani, and Steven Davidoff Solomon, "The New Titans of Wall Street: A Theoretical Framework for Passive Investors," *University of Pennsylvania Law Review* 168 (2019): 17–72.
6. Edward Rock and Marcel Kahan, "Index Funds and Corporate Governance: Let Shareholders be Shareholders" (April 4, 2019). NYU Law and Economics Research Paper No. 18-39, http://dx.doi.org/10.2139/ssrn.3295098.
7. Fisch et al., "The New Titans of Wall Street."
8. Tom Gayner, Washington Post Co. director, interview with author, October 21, 2018.
9. Peter Iliev, Jonathan Kalodimos, and Michelle Lowry, "Investors' Attention to Corporate Governance," March 6, 2019 (unpublished manuscript), https://ssrn.com/abstract=3162407.
10. Lucian Bebchuk and Scott Hirst, "Index Funds and the Future of Corporate Governance: Theory, Evidence, and Policy," *Columbia Law Review* 119 (2019): 2029–146.
11. James R. Copland, David F. Larcker, and Brian Tayan, "Proxy Advisory Firms: Empirical Evidence and the Case for Reform," Manhattan Institute, New York, May 21, 2018, https://www.scribd.com/document/379744291/Proxy-Advisory-Firms-Empirical-Evidence-and-the-Case-for-Reform; Stephen Choi, Jill Fisch, and Marcel Kahan, "The Power of Proxy Advisory Firms: Myth or Reality?," *Emory Law Journal* 59 (2010): 869–918

(distinguishing correlation and causation); Christie Hayne and Marshall D. Vance, "Information Intermediary or De Facto Standard Setter? Field Evidence on the Indirect and Direct Influence of Proxy Advisors," *Journal of Accounting Research*, (forthcoming), https://ssrn.com/abstract=3325622 (boards "succumb to [proxy advisor] influence by making changes to their compensation design both before and in response to proxy voting"); Paul Rose, "The Corporate Governance Industry," *Journal of Corporation Law* 32, no. 4 (2007): 887–926 ("ISS advice has been cited as a decisive factor in a number of major corporate events.").

12. James R. Copland, David F. Larcker, and Brian Tayan, "The Big Thumb on the Scale: An Overview of the Proxy Advisory Industry," Stanford Closer Look Series, Stanford Business Graduate School, Stanford, Calif., May 30, 2018, https://www.gsb.stanford.edu/faculty-research/publications /big-thumb-scale-overview-proxy-advisory-industry.

13. See "UBS French Tax Fine 'Serious Concern,' Shareholder Adviser Says," *Bloomberg*, April 15, 2019, https://news.bloombergtax.com/daily -tax-report-international/ubs-french-tax-fine-serious-concern-shareholder -adviser-says.

14. See, e.g., Jason Zweig, "Like Buffett, Another Folksy Investor Turns Patience into Profit," *Wall Street Journal*, May 22, 2015.

15. See Bernard S. Black, "Agents Watching Agents: The Promise of Institutional Investor Voice," *UCLA Law Review* 39 (1992): 811–93.

16. Jeff Stagl, "CSX/TCI Proxy Fight Goes an Extra Round," *Progressive Railroading*, July 2008.

17. Other close votes have come on executive compensation, including one that failed by a nose at Merck (garnering 49.2 percent) and another that squeaked by at Verizon (50.2 percent). Although most mergers sail through with shareholder approval, there have been some close calls, including of less than 2 percent for those of Compaq–HP and AXA–MONY.

18. See Alon Brav, Wei Jiang, and Tao Li, "Picking Friends Before Picking (Proxy) Fights: How Mutual Fund Voting Shapes Proxy Contests," Columbia Business School Research Paper No. 18–16; European Corporate Governance Institute (ECGI)—Finance Working Paper No. 601/2019, https://papers.ssrn.com/sol3/papers.cfm?abstract_id=3101473.

19. Thomas Buckley and Scott Deveau, "Singer's Elliott Pounces on World's Second-Largest Distiller," *Bloomberg*, December 12, 2018.

20. See Austen Hufford, "3M Sticks Together as Rivals Break Up," *Wall Street Journal*, April 11, 2019.

21. Among these: State Farm (nearly 3 percent of its portfolio representing almost 2 percent of the company); Massachusetts Financial (1 percent and 2 percent, respectively); Wellington (0.4 percent and 1.4 percent);

U.S. Bancorp (2.8 percent and 0.8 percent); First Eagle (2.3 percent and 0.7 percent); and Fundsmith (more than 4 percent and 0.6 percent).

22. UTX made a substantial acquisition as part of its defense-contracting business housing Pratt & Whitney by acquiring Rockwell Collins in the largest acquisition in the aerospace industry's history. Then it announced the spin-offs of its elevator and air conditioner businesses, Otis and Carrier, respectively. Measured by approximate annual revenues, the combined aerospace business (now called Collins) runs to $40 billion, with Carrier at $18 billion and Otis at $12 billion. Then UTX announced a merger with Raytheon, to be followed by the divestiture of all non-aerospace businesses.

23. Among these: Barrow Hanley (2.38 percent of its portfolio and 1.34 percent of the stock); Davis Selected Advisers (4.93 and 1.02); Boston Partners (1.07 and 0.83); Massachusetts Financial (0.87 and 1.89); Capital Research (0.34 and 1.06); AKO Capital (4.93 and 0.09); Southeastern (4.65 and 0.35); and Burgundy (4.40 and 0.42).

24. Stephen Singer, "Large UTC Shareholder Slams Proposed Raytheon Merger as 'Irresponsible,' " *Hartford Courant*, June 28, 2019 (indicating that UTC responded to Loeb's criticism saying other shareholders endorse the transactions).

25. Thomas Gryta and Dave Sebastain, "United Tech Says Deals Will Pay Off," *Wall Street Journal*, July 24, 2019.

3. Competitive Advantages

1. Michael E. Porter, *Competitive Strategy: Techniques for Analyzing Industries and Competitors* (New York: Free Press, 1980).

2. Brian L. Connelly, Laszlo Tihanyi, S. Trevis Certo, and Michael A. Hitt, "Marching to the Beat of Different Drummers: The Influence of Institutional Owners on Competitive Actions," *Academy of Management Journal* 53 (2010): 723–42.

3. The cultivation of QSs as a management practice producing competitive advantage is akin to management practices embracing business methods as moats, such as Six Sigma and the Toyota Production System, which relentlessly reduce manufacturing error; just-in-time inventory that minimizes the cost of working capital; and autonomous decentralized organizational structures that maximize employee potential.

4. Markel Corporation, "Letter to Shareholders," *Annual Report*, 2018, http://www.annualreports.com/HostedData/AnnualReports/PDF/NYSE _MKL_2018.pdf.

5. See Allen C. Benello, Michael Van Biema, and Tobias E. Carlisle, *Concentrated Investing* (Hoboken: Wiley, 2017), 78–82, citing William Poundstone, *Fortune's Formula: The Untold Story of the Scientific Betting System that Beat the Casinos and Wall Street* (New York: Farrar, Straus and Giroux, 2006).

6. See Jimmy Soni and Rob Goodman, *A Mind at Play: How Claude Shannon Invented the Information Age* (New York: Simon and Schuster, 2017).

7. See Ralph Vartabedian, "Singleton Gives up His Chief Executive Title at Teledyne," *Los Angeles Times*, April 24, 1986.

8. See James Flanigan, "Teledyne Likely to Try Winning Formula Again," *Los Angeles Times*, May 1, 1987, https://www.latimes.com/archives/la-xpm -1987-05-01-fi-1888-story.htm (noting that Sarofim owned 8.7 percent of Teledyne's stock); Rocket Financial, Fayez Sarofim & Co., Public Holdings, https://www.rocketfinancial.com/OwnHist.aspx?sID=3633&fID=16788 (tabulating public filings indicating that the firm has held about 100,000 Teledyne shares from at least 2004 through the present).

9. See Doron Levin and Bradford Marion, "21st Century Solutions to Selling Cars," *Korn Ferry Institute Briefings Magazine*, February 24, 2016.

10. See "Letter of Donald Graham to Shareholders of The Washington Post Co." (2003), reprinted in Lawrence A. Cunningham, *Dear Shareholder* (Petersfield: Harriman House, 2020).

11. Warren Buffett, "The Superinvestors of Graham and Doddsville," *Hermes*, 1984.

12. The examples of Dell and AOL–Time Warner are inspired by the treatment in Baruch Lev, *Winning Investors Over* (Brighton, Mass.: Harvard Business Review, 2011).

13. David D. Kirkpatrick and David Carr, "A Media Giant Needs a Script," *New York Times*, July 7, 2002.

14. See Prem C. Jain, "The Effect on Stock Price of Inclusion in or Exclusion from the S&P 500," *Financial Analysts Journal* 43, no. 1 (1987): 58–65.

15. Antti Petajisto, "The Index Premium and Its Hidden Cost for Index Funds," *Journal of Empirical Finance* 18, no. 2 (2011): 272; Andrei Shleifer, "Do Demand Curves for Stocks Slope Down?," *Journal of Finance* 41, no. 3 (1986): 584; William B. Elliott, Bonnie F. Van Ness, Mark D. Walker, and Richard S. Warral, "What Drives the S&P 500 Inclusion Effect? An Analytical Survey," *Financial Management* 35, no. 4 (2006): 31–2.

16. Pyemo N. Afego, "Effects of Changes in Stock Index Compositions: A Literature Survey," *International Financial Analysis* 52 (2017): 239.

17. See Scott Hirst and Kobi Kastiel, "Corporate Governance by Index Exclusion," *Boston University Law Review* 99 (2019): 1229–78.

18. See Paul Borochin and Jie Yang, "The Effects of Institutional Investor Objectives on Firm Valuation and Governance," *Journal of Financial*

Economics 126, no. 1 (2017): 171–99. Other recent research affirms other advantages that long-term investors contribute to companies they invest in. Jarrad Harford, Ambrus Kecksés, and Sattar Mansi, "Do Long-Term Investors Improve Corporate Decision Making?" (conference paper, Finance Down Under 2015: Building on the Best from the Cellars of Finance Paper, Asian Finance Association, Melbourne, Australia, March 5–7, 2015), SSRN abstract_id=2505261.

19. See Michael J. Mauboussin and Dan Callahan, "Measuring the Moat," Credit Suisse, July 22, 2013, http://csinvesting.org/wp-content/uploads/2013/07/Measuring_the_Moat_July2013.pdf.

20. The list of the top 100 brand managers is taken from Brand Finance, "Brand Guardianship Index," in Global 500 2019 (January 2019), 36–37, https://brandfinance.com/images/upload/global_500_2019_locked_4.pdf. It is compared to Cunningham, QS Density Ranking (described in appendix A). Of the 38 U.S. managers on the Brand Guardian Index, 36 of them are on the QS Density Ranking.

4. The Corporate Message

1. Warren E. Buffett and Lawrence A. Cunningham, *The Essays of Warren Buffett: Lessons for Corporate America*, 5th ed. (Durham, NC: Carolina Academic Press, 2019), 30–36.

2. A substantial excerpt follows (omissions are not indicated by ellipses):

We believe our first responsibility is to the patients, doctors and nurses, to mothers and fathers and all others who use our products and services. We must constantly strive to provide value, reduce our costs and maintain reasonable prices. Our business partners must have an opportunity to make a fair profit.

We are responsible to our employees who work with us throughout the world. We must provide an inclusive work environment where each person must be considered as an individual. We must respect their diversity and dignity and recognize their merit. We must support the health and well-being of our employees and help them fulfill their family and other personal responsibilities. We must provide highly capable leaders and their actions must be just and ethical.

We are responsible to the communities in which we live and work and to the world community as well. We must help people be healthier by supporting better access and care in more places around the world.

We must be good citizens—support good works and charities, better health and education, and bear our fair share of taxes. We must maintain in good order the property we are privileged to use, protecting the environment and natural resources.

Our final responsibility is to our stockholders. Business must make a sound profit. We must experiment with new ideas. Research must be carried on, innovative programs developed, investments made for the future and mistakes paid for. New equipment must be purchased, new facilities provided and new products launched. Reserves must be created to provide for adverse times. When we operate according to these principles, the stockholders should realize a fair return.

3. A substantial excerpt follows (omissions are not indicated by ellipses):

We believe the free-market system is the best means of generating good jobs, a strong and sustainable economy, innovation, a healthy environment and economic opportunity for all. Businesses play a vital role. While each of our individual companies serves its own corporate purpose, we share a fundamental commitment to all of our stakeholders. We commit to:

- Delivering value to our customers. We will further the tradition of American companies leading the way in meeting or exceeding customer expectations.
- Investing in our employees. This starts with compensating them fairly and providing important benefits. It also includes supporting them through training and education that help develop new skills for a rapidly changing world. We foster diversity and inclusion, dignity and respect.
- Dealing fairly and ethically with our suppliers. We are dedicated to serving as good partners to the other companies, large and small, that help us meet our missions.
- Supporting the communities in which we work. We respect the people in our communities and protect the environment by embracing sustainable practices across our businesses.
- Generating long-term value for shareholders, who provide the capital that allows companies to invest, grow and innovate. We are committed to transparency and effective engagement with shareholders.

Each of our stakeholders is essential. We commit to deliver value to all of them, for the future success of our companies, our communities and our country.

4. This assertion is based on comparing the companies signatory to the Business Roundtable mission statement to Cunningham, QS Density Ranking (described in appendix A). Of the 183 signatories, 135 are on the QS Density Ranking. Among those, one-third are in the top 10 percent of the QS Density Ranking; 55 percent are in the top quarter; and 81 percent are in the top half.

Consider further the management leadership rankings by the Drucker Institute of S&P 500 companies according to principles associated with its namesake, the management professor, Peter Drucker. Notably, the Drucker Institute studied the relation between Business Roundtable signatories and the institute's overall rankings, finding relations parallel to those found between such signatories and QS density. Rick Wartzman and Kelly Tang, "The Business Roundtable's Model of Capitalism Does Pay Off," *Wall Street Journal*, October 27, 2019. Such an association also appeared between the Drucker Institute's highest-ranked companies and high QS density. The QS Density Ranking contained 141 companies appearing among the Drucker 2018 list of the top 150 companies. Of these, 28 percent of the Drucker 150 is in the top 10 percent of the QS Density Ranking; 54 percent is in the top quarter; and 84 percent is in the top half. See appendix A.

5. Adapted from Denis Kreft, "31 Amazing (and a Few Awful) Company Mission Statement Examples You Can Sink Your Teeth Into," *Imaginasium* (blog), https://imaginasium.com/blog/company-mission-statement-examples-business.

6. This assertion relates the companies boasting strong mission statements to Cunningham, QS Density Ranking (described in appendix A).

5. Annual Letters

1. Elizabeth J. Howell-Hanano, "Pearls of Wisdom: The Best Shareholder Letters Nobody Is Reading," Toptal, November 7, 2017, https://www.toptal.com/finance/equity-research-analysts/best-shareholder-letters (study of all companies in the S&P 600 small cap index).

2. See Laura Rittenhouse, *Investing Between the Lines: How to Make Smarter Decisions by Decoding CEO Communications* (New York: McGraw Hill Professional, 2013).

3. See Eric R. Heyman, "What You Can Learn from Shareholder Letters," *American Association of Individual Investors Journal*, October 2010 (recommending studying a company's shareholder letter with as much care as its financials, looking for general adequacy of explanations spanning from financial strength to addressing economic challenges).

4. Email from Mark Hughes to the author, August 27, 2018.

5. John Train, *Money Masters of Our Time* (New York: HarperCollins, 2000), 223.

6. See Rittenhouse Rankings, "Companies Excelling in Rittenhouse Candor Analytics™ Substantially Outperform the Market in 2016," press release, December 13, 2016. The assertion in the text is based on comparing the listing in Rittenhouse Rankings to the QS density rankings contained in Cunningham, QS Density Ranking (described in appendix A).

6. Annual Meetings

1. Randy Cepuch, *A Weekend with Warren Buffett and Other Shareholder Meeting Adventures* (New York: Basic Books, 2007), 211.

2. This paragraph is adapted from Robert E. Denham, "The Shareholders You Deserve," in *The Warren Buffett Shareholder: Stories from Inside the Berkshire Hathaway Annual Meeting*, ed. Lawrence A. Cunningham and Stephanie Cuba (New York: Harriman, 2018), 171.

3. John Brooks, "Stockholder Season," *New Yorker*, October 8, 1966.

4. Adapted from Lawrence A. Cunningham and Stephanie Cuba, *Shareholder Annual Meetings, Financial History* (2018).

5. Michael D. Reagan, "What 17 Million Shareholders Share," *New York Times*, February 23, 1964.

6. See Lawrence A. Cunningham and Stephanie Cuba, *The Warren Buffett Shareholder: Stories from the Berkshire Hathaway Annual Meeting* (2018) (illuminating essays by forty denizens of the Berkshire shareholder meeting, including Tom Gayner, Robert Hagstrom, Robert Miles, and Tom Russo, who collectively had attended the meeting 750 times).

7. See Cepuch, *A Weekend with Warren Buffett and Other Shareholder Meeting Adventures*.

8. Cepuch, *A Weekend with Warren Buffett and Other Shareholder Meeting Adventures*, 191.

9. Cepuch, *A Weekend with Warren Buffett and Other Shareholder Meeting Adventures*, 120.

10. Cepuch, *A Weekend with Warren Buffett and Other Shareholder Meeting Adventures*, 163.

11. See Cepuch, *A Weekend with Warren Buffett and Other Shareholder Meeting Adventures*, 190–191.

12. Cepuch, *A Weekend with Warren Buffett and Other Shareholder Meeting Adventures*, 141.

13. Both federal and stock exchange rules defer to state law on the manner of holding annual meetings.

14. The assertions in this paragraph rank companies involved in public discussions of the format of their annual meeting in relation to Cunningham, QS Density Ranking (described in appendix A).

15. Cepuch, *A Weekend with Warren Buffett and Other Shareholder Meeting Adventures*, 225.

7. Quality Quarterly Contact

1. See Lawrence A. Cunningham, "Finance Theory and Accounting Fraud: Fantastic Futures Versus Conservative Histories," *Buffalo Law Review* 53, no. 3 (2005): 789–814.

2. These points are inspired by the shareholder letters by Charles Fabrikant of SEACOR and Don Graham of the Washington Post Co.

3. Loews Corporation letter, 2007.

4. See John R. Graham, Campbell R. Harvey, and Shivaram Rajgopal, "The Economic Implications of Corporate Financial Reporting," *Journal of Accounting and Economics* 40, nos. 1–3 (2005): 3–73.

5. A 2006 article by McKinsey & Co. researchers reported a plateau around 2001 in the number of companies maintaining the practice (about twelve hundred or four thousand companies surveyed) accompanied by a steadily increasing number of companies ending their former practice of providing quarterly guidance, a figure exceeding two hundred by 2004. Peggy Hsieh, Timothy Koller, and S. R. Rajan, "The Misguided Practice of Earnings Guidance," *McKinsey & Co. Strategy & Corporate Finance* (March 2006), https://www.mckinsey.com/business-functions/strategy-and-corporate-finance/our-insights/the-misguided-practice-of-earnings-guidance. On the other hand, in 2017, S&P Global Market Intelligence reported that 146 companies of the S&P 500 provided earnings guidance that year, the highest number in a decade. See Stephen Grocer, "Quarterly Guidance," *New York Times*, September 26, 2018.

6. Yongtae Kim et al., "Does the Cessation of Quarterly Earnings Guidance Reduce Investors' Short-Termism?," *Review of Accounting Studies* 22, no. 2 (2017): 715–22; see also Shuping Chen, Dawn A. Matsumoto, and Shivaram Rajgopal, "Is Silence Golden? An Empirical Analysis of Firms That Stop Giving Quarterly Earnings Guidance in the Post Regulation-FD Period," *Journal of Accounting and Economics* 51, no. 1–2 (2011): 134–50.

7. See Lex Suvanto, "Should Boards of Directors Communicate with Shareholders?," *IR Magazine*, January 2015.

8. See Susanne Craig and Jessica Silver-Greenberg, "JP Morgan Works to Avert Split of Chief and Chairman Roles," *New York Times*, April 5, 2013.

9. Jonathan M. Karpoff, Robert J. Schonlau and Katsushi Suzuki, "Shareholder Perks, Ownership Structure, and Firm Value," Working Paper, 2015/2018, available at https://papers.ssrn.com/sol3/papers.cfm?abstract_id=2615777.

10. See chapter 3 and table 3-1 , noting data relating leading brand managers to relative QS density.

11. The assertions in this paragraph relate companies offering shareholder rewards programs to the company rankings by shareholder quality summarized in Cunningham, QS Density Ranking (described in appendix A).

12. Michael McDonald, "11 Hidden Perks of Owning Stocks," GOBankingRates.com, November 24, 2015, https://www.nasdaq.com/articles/11 -hidden-perks-owning-stocks-2015-11-24.

13. Kimberly Clark's shareholder rewards programs have personal resonance. When I was a child, my grandmother, a Kimberly Clark shareholder, always gave our family a Christmas gift box with many Kimberly Clark products. The tradition led me as an adult to buy the stock, which I held for many years.

Some major French companies, such as L'Oreal Group and Air Liquide, go further. They reward longer-term shareholders with enhanced dividends or voting rights, attracting individual and institutional owners alike. See Barry B. Burr, "Mercer Seeks Long-Term Shareholder Rewards Program from Corporations," *Pensions & Investments*, December 6, 2012.

14. See Broadridge and PwC, *Proxy Pulse*, 2019 edition, https://www .broadridge.com/proxypulse.

8. Useful Metrics

1. The Drucker quote is sometimes attributed to Lord Kelvin; see Louis Lowenstein, "Financial Transparency and Corporate Governance: You Manage What You Measure," *Columbia Law Review* 96 (1996): 1335–62.

2. The assertions in this paragraph are based on a search of all 10K reports from 1996 through 2018. The term "economic profit" appeared 641 times in filings of some two hundred different companies. Limiting the search to those companies with at least seven instances, twenty companies appeared—half continuing to use the term through the present, including Coca-Cola and Credit Acceptance; its use by the other half having ceased at some point in the recent past.

Six of the ten continuing companies rank in the top third of QSs, with only one in the bottom half, along with a few outside the rankings.

Among companies that ceased using the term, only two are in the top third, while two are in the bottom half, and most are unranked. Among the unranked are mostly smaller companies, although one's cessation coincided with the discovery of the company's involvement in unsavory or illegal business activities.

Some other notable companies appearing on the original but not the modified list include 3M (1998–2001); Boeing (2000–2002); Eastman Kodak (2002–2003, notable due to its ignominious fate amid the digital revolution); and XTRA (1997–2000, notable because it was acquired in 2001 by Berkshire Hathaway).

3. See Seanna Asper, Chris McCoy, and Gary K. Taylor, "The Expanding Use of Non-GAAP Financial Measures: Understanding Their Utility and Regulatory Limitations," *CPA Journal*, July 2019.

4. See Amanda Iacone, "SEC Flags Cash-Flow Measure That Made WeWork Look Profitable," *Bloomberg*, December 3, 2019.

5. See Howard Schilit, "Do Ride-Sharing Customers Sit in Front?," *Wall Street Journal*, April 28, 2019.

6. Brian Bushee, "Identifying and Attracting the 'Right' Investors," *Journal of Applied Corporate Finance* 16, no. 4 (2004): 33.

9. Capital Allocation

1. See George Athanassakos, "Do Value Investor CEOs Outperform?" (Working paper, Western University, April 20, 2020), an empirical study ranking companies based on the capital allocation skills of their CEOs. The assertion in the text is based on comparing the companies identified by Professor Athanassakos to Cunningham, QS Density Ranking (described in Appendix A). Of the 167 companies identified by Professor Athanassakos, 140 are on the QS Density Ranking. Among those, 26 percent are in the top 10 percent of the QSDR, 56 percent are in the top quarter, and 75 percent are in the top half.

2. See Phil Ordway, "Case Studies of Companies That Do Capital Allocation Right," The Manual of Ideas, January 15, 2019, https://moiglobal.com /phil-ordway-201901/?.

3. See Mark Leonard, "Letter to Constellation Software Shareholders," 2006, 2007.

4. See Loews' letter to shareholders, 2013.

5. See Michael J. Barclay and Clifford W. Smith, "Corporate Payout Policy: Cash Dividends Versus Open Market Share Repurchases," *Journal*

of Financial Economics 22, no. 1 (1988): 61–82 (while 81 percent of NYSE firms paid dividends from 1983 to 1986, less than 12 percent conducted share buybacks).

6. The legendary Teledyne executive, Henry Singleton (1916–1999), is considered an all-star for shareholder buybacks, as Prem Watsa noted in 1997:

> Henry began Teledyne in 1961 with approximately seven million shares outstanding and grew the company through acquisitions while shares outstanding peaked in 1972 at 88 million. From 1972 to 1987, long before stock buybacks became popular, Henry reduced the shares outstanding by 87 percent to 12 million. Book value per share and stock prices compounded in excess of 22 percent per year during Henry's 27-year watch at Teledyne—one of the best track records in the business.

7. See Ordway, "Case Studies of Companies That Do Capital Allocation Right."

8. Peter Lynch, *One Up on Wall Street* (New York: Simon and Schuster, 1989).

9. E.g., Delaware General Corporation Law 154 (dividends), 160 (repurchases technically do not explicitly require board approval but statutory rules violations expose directors to personal liability), and 251 (mergers).

10. See Ordway, "Case Studies of Companies That Do Capital Allocation Right."

10. Trackers and Spins

1. This section on trackers is adapted from Lawrence A. Cunningham and Patrick T. Brennan, "Tracking Stocks: Rise, Fall, Revival," *Financial History* 123 (Fall 2017).

2. See Stephen I. Glover, *Business Separation Transactions: Spin-Offs, Subsidiary IPOs and Tracking Stock* (Philadelphia: Law Journal Press, 2018).

3. Specifically, Third Point acquired 2.25 million Danaher shares in late 2015, increased to 4.5 million by late 2016, before selling down to 3.25 million held through late 2018—the latter representing 0.46 percent of the company's outstanding shares.

4. These included Capital Research Global Investors (0.32 percent of its portfolio for 1.46 percent of Danaher); Brown Advisory (2.11 and 0.98);

Findlay Park (3.53 and 0.49); Blue Ridge Capital (2.39 and 0.34); and Ruane Cunniff (0.75 and 0.21).

5. See Kate Welling and Mario Gabelli, *Merger Masters* (New York: Columbia University Press, 2018).

11. Director Selection: Stewards, Advocates, or Walkovers?

1. See Lawrence A. Cunningham, "Warren Buffett's Ten Commandments for Directors," *NACD Directorship*, July–August 2017.

2. John H. Matheson and Vilena Nicolet, "Shareholder Democracy and Special Interest Governance," *Minnesota Law Review* 103 (2019): 1649–96.

3. Lucian Bebchuk and Scott Hirst, "Index Funds and the Future of Corporate Governance: Theory, Evidence, and Policy," *Columbia Law Review* 119 (2019): 2029–146.

4. Jill E. Fisch, Assaf Hamdani, and Steven Davidoff Solomon, "The New Titans of Wall Street: A Theoretical Framework for Passive Investors," *University of Pennsylvania Law Review* 168 (2019): 17–72.

5. E.g., Sanjai Bhagat and Bernard Black, "The Non-correlation Between Board Independence and Long-Term Firm Performance," *Journal of Corporation Law* 27 (2002): 231–73; Benjamin E. Hermalin and Michael S. Weisbach, "Boards of Directors as an Endogenously Determined Institution: A Survey of the Economic Literature," *Federal Reserve Bank of New York Economic Policy Review* 9, no. 1 (2003): 7–26; Lawrence A. Cunningham, "Rediscovering Board Expertise: Legal Implications of the Empirical Literature," *University of Cincinnati Law Review* 77 (2008): 465–99; Usha Rodrigues, "The Fetishization of Independence," *Journal of Corporation Law* 33, no. 2 (2008): 447–96.

6. The assertions in this paragraph are based on comparing data on companies with and without split chair–CEO functions to Cunningham, QS Density Ranking (described in appendix A). For instance, within the S&P 500, 229 split and 245 combine the roles; of these, 216 and 234, respectively, appear in the QSDR. Of those splitting, 16 percent are in the top 10 percent, 40 percent in the top 25 percent, and 89 percent in the top 50 percent; of those combining, 28 percent are in the top 10 percent, 57 percent in the top 25 percent, and 84 percent in the top 50 percent.

7. See K. J. Martijn Cremers and Simone M. Sepe, "The Shareholder Value of Empowered Boards," *Stanford Law Review* 68, no. 1 (2016): 67–148.

8. See Bebchuk and Hirst, "Index Funds and the Future of Corporate Governance" (indicating that about half the Russell 3000 companies have

staggered boards). According to Wharton Research Data Services (WRDS), within the S&P 500, 61 companies have staggered boards. Comparing these 61 and a random sample of 61 with unitary boards to Cunningham, QS Density Ranking (described in appendix A), 14 percent of the staggered board companies are in the top 10 percent of quality shareholder density vs. 37 percent of the unitary board company sample in the top 10 percent.

9. A final plank in ISS's accountability platform prescribes that each board undertake regular performance reviews of itself. This is another fashion in corporate governance that is reinforced by consulting firms offering the service. Christopher D. McKenna, *The World's Newest Profession: Management Consulting in the Twentieth Century*, Cambridge Studies in the Emergence of Global Enterprise (Cambridge: Cambridge University Press, 2006). The task of self-evaluation, while important, is challenging, and observers are justified in skepticism about the results.

10. Bebchuk and Hirst, "Index Funds and the Future of Corporate Governance."

11. Fisch, Hamdani, and Solomon, "The New Titans of Wall Street."

12. Fisch, Hamdani, and Solomon, "The New Titans of Wall Street."

13. Ronald J. Gilson and Jeffrey N. Gordon, "The Agency Costs of Activism," *Columbia Law Review* 113 (2013): 863–928.

14. See Rima Ramchandani and David A. Seville, "Gender Diversity in Corporate Canada: Canada's Securities Regulators Publish 2014–2018 Statistics," *Torys LLP*, September 28, 2018; see also Statistics Canada, "CSA Multilateral Staff Notice 58–310 Report on Fourth Staff Review of Disclosure Regarding Women on Boards and in Executive Officer Positions," last modified February 6, 2020, https://www.statcan.gc.ca/eng/topics-start /gender_diversity_and_inclusion?HPA=1.

15. See Dawn Calleja, Steve Bearton, and Joanna Pachner, "It's 2019: Where Are All the Women in Corporate Canada?," *Globe and Mail*, May 31, 2019 (reporting data from the Rothman School of 289 TSX companies on: [1] percent of female directors, rising from less than 10 percent in 2008 to 13.1 percent in 2013 to 24 percent in 2018 and [2] boards by number of female directors today with 32 percent at one, 28 percent at two, and 22 percent at three).

16. Yaron Nili, "Beyond the Numbers: Substantive Gender Diversity in Boardrooms," *Indiana Law Journal* 94, no. 1 (2019): 145–202.

17. See Aaron A. Dhir, *Challenging Boardroom Homogeneity* (Cambridge: Cambridge University Press, 2015), reviewed by Amanda K. Packel, "Government Intervention into Board Composition: Gender Quotas in Norway and Diversity Disclosures in the United States," review of *Challenging Boardroom Homogeneity* by Aaron A. Dhir, *Stanford Journal of Law, Business, and Finance* 21, no. 2 (2016): 192–239.

18. Deborah Rhode and Amanda K. Packel, "Diversity on Corporate Boards: How Much Difference Does It Make?," *Delaware Journal of Corporate Law* 39, no. 2 (2014): 377–426. See also Renee B. Adams and Daniel Ferreira, "Women in the Boardroom and Their Impact on Governance and Performance," *Journal of Financial Economics* 94 (2009): 291–309; Darren Rosenblum and Daria Roithmayr, "More Than a Woman: Insights Into Corporate Governance After the French Sex Quota," *Indiana Law Review* 48, no. 3 (2015): 889–930.

19. See note 5 above.

20. 2020 Women on Boards, "Working Hard to Raise the Bar," September 2019, https://2020wob.com/wp-content/uploads/2019/10/2020WOB_Gender_Diversity_Index_Report_Oct2019.pdf.

21. See The 2020 Women on Boards' Honor Roll Companies for 2017, which includes 176 companies that have been Winning "W" Companies for seven consecutive years, 2011–2017, https://www.2020wob.com/companies/2013-honor-roll-companies.

12. Managerial Performance: The Overpaid and Underpaid

1. In re The Walt Disney Company, 906 A.2d 27 (Del. 2006).

2. See Rogers v. Hill, 289 U.S. 582 (1933).

3. See Erik Lie, "On the Timing of CEO Stock Option Awards," *Management Science* 51 (May 2005): 802.

4. See Maurice Greenberg and Lawrence A. Cunningham, *The AIG Story* (Hoboken, N.J.: Wiley, 2013).

5. Recipients were covered by the pay rules until all debts were repaid. The Emergency Economic Stabilization Act of 2008 (EESA), as amended by the American Recovery and Reinvestment Act of 2009 (ARRA).

6. Mary Williams Walshjan, "U.S. Faulted Over Pay at Rescued Firms," *New York Times*, January 24, 2012.

7. See Janet McFarland, "Is Options Accounting a Legal Case," *Globe and Mail*, November 13, 2002 (discussing extensive legal research reaching that conclusion by the Toronto law firm of McDonald & Hayden at the request of noted investor Steve Scotchmer).

8. This is based on comparing the companies found to pay nominal executive salaries to the QS density rankings contained in Cunningham, QS Density Ranking (described in appendix A). Notably, of the few dozen SEC registrants appearing on the annual entry at least five times, nine are from a single sector: real estate investment trusts (REITs). Virtually all these REITs engaged

external management companies. As a result, their own executives are paid by such firms rather than by the REITs. For many in this cohort, therefore, the modest salary is essentially meaningless. Some may even draw criticism from many QSs who are critical of the externally managed REIT structure. In a proxy contest mounted by Sessa Capital, a QS of an externally managed REIT, Ashford Hospitality Prime, I served as a director nominee for nearly two years of battle and eventually served a short term as a member of the Ashford board.

13. Shareholder Voting: One Each, Dual Class, or Quality?

1. See Joel Seligman, "Equal Protection in Shareholder Voting Rights: The One Common Share, One Vote Controversy," *George Washington Law Review* 54 (1986), 687; Joseph A. Livingston, *The American Stockholder* (Philadelphia: Lippincott, 1958), 186–87; Robert Sobel, *The Big Board* (New York: Free Press, 1965), 236.

2. See John C. Coffee, "The Rise of Dispersed Ownership: The Roles of Law and the State in the Separation of Ownership and Control," *Yale Law Journal* 111, no. 1 (2001): 1–82.

3. See Scott Hirst and Kobi Kastiel, "Corporate Governance by Index Exclusion," *Boston University Law Review* 99 (2019): 1229–78.

4. See Council of Institutional Investors, "Dual Class Companies List" (2017), https://www.cii.org/files/3_17_17_List_of_DC_for_Website(1).pdf (culled from Russell 3000 companies).

5. See Jill Fisch and Steven Davidoff Solomon, "The Problem of Sunsets," *Boston University Law Review* 99 (2019): 1057–94.

6. See Council of Institutional Investors, "Dual-Class IPO Snapshot: 2017–2019 Statistics," https://www.cii.org/files/2019%20Dual%20Class%20Update%20for%20Website%20FINAL(2).pdf.

7. It is also possible to construct an across-the-board case endorsing dual-class capital structures. See Dorothy S. Lund, "Nonvoting Shares and Efficient Corporate Governance," *Stanford Law Review* 71, no. 3 (2019): 687–745.

8. See Council of Institutional Investors, "Dual Class Companies List" (2017).

9. Comparing the CII's list of 225 companies with Cunningham, QS Density Ranking (described in appendix A), 135 companies appear on both lists. Among those, 64 percent appeared in the top half for QS density.

10. A credible argument exists that indexers should not be entitled to any vote. See Dorothy S. Lund, "The Case Against Passive Shareholder Voting," *Journal of Corporation Law* 43, no. 3 (2018): 493–536.

11. See David J. Berger, Steven Davidoff Solomon, and Aaron J. Benjamin, "Tenure Voting and the U.S. Public Company," *Business Lawyer* 72 (2017): 295–324.

12. The Delaware Supreme Court upheld the validity of a charter amendment adopting time-weighted voting in Williams v. Geier, 671 A.2d 1368 (1996).

13. This assertion is based on the empirical analysis described in appendix A.

14. Francois Belot, Edith Ginglinger, and Laura T. Starks, "Encouraging Long-Term Shareholders: The Effects of Loyalty Shares with Double Voting Rights," Université Paris-Dauphine Research Paper No. 3475429, Proceedings of the Paris December 2019 Finance Meeting EUROFIDAI—ESSEC (2019), www.ssrn.com/abstract=3475429.

15. Lynne Dallas and Jordan Barry, "Long-Term Shareholders and Time-Phased Voting," *Delaware Journal of Corporate Law* 40, no. 2 (2015): 541–646.

16. Todd M. Henderson and Dorothy S. Lund, "Index Funds Are Great for Investors, Risky for Corporate Governance," *Wall Street Journal*, June 22, 2017; Lund, "The Case Against Passive Shareholder Voting."

17. E.g., Lucian A. Bebchuk and Scott Hirst, "Index Funds and the Future of Corporate Governance: Theory, Evidence, and Policy," *Columbia Law Review* 119 (2019): 2029–2145; Jill E. Fisch, Assaf Hamdani, and Steven Davidoff Solomon, "The New Titans of Wall Street: A Theoretical Framework for Passive Investors," *University of Pennsylvania Law Review* 168 (2019): 17–72.

18. Sean J. Griffith, "Opt-In Stewardship: Toward an Optimal Delegation of Mutual Fund Voting Authority," *Texas Law Review* 98 (2020).

19. Eric Posner and E. Glen Weyl, "Quadratic Vote Buying as Efficient Corporate Governance," *University of Chicago Law Review* 81, no. 1 (2014): 251–72.

20. Corporate laws permit such voting alternatives, with shareholder approval. Current stock exchange listing standards may need waiving to accommodate them. New York Stock Exchange limitations on voting rule changes can be read to permit amendment of a listed company's charter to adopt time-weighted voting rules. See Berger, Solomon, and Benjamin, "Tenure Voting and the U.S. Public Company," (rule forbids "disparately" reducing voting rights, whereas switching to a time-weighted voting is nondisparate, because it is equally applicable to all shares held for stated durations).

More experimentally, voting rules could measure shareholder quality by portfolio rather than particular company. A QS is a QS, even when first buying stock in a new company. At least initially, added voting rights could be based on an investor's historical average holding periods or concentration levels.

Epilogue: Getting Indexers and Activists Going Quality

1. Jill E. Fisch, Assaf Hamdani, and Steven Davidoff Solomon, "The New Titans of Wall Street: A Theoretical Framework for Passive Investors," *University of Pennsylvania Law Review* 168 (2019): 17–72.

2. Lucian Bebchuk and Scott Hirst, "Index Funds and the Future of Corporate Governance: Theory, Evidence, and Policy," *Columbia Law Review* 119 (2019): 2029–146.

3. Some (rhetorical) questions: Can transients be encouraged to slow down? Would curtailing quarterly guidance and conference calls help? Will insistence on reporting results as they come—not smoothing things out—induce a longer view over multiple quarters and years rather than the latest one?

Can indexers be trained in capital allocation—and to grade it in particular companies? Can indexers dispense with broad abstract statements of rigid director attributes and focus more on experience, judgment, wisdom, and concern for the particular company?

Might revisiting voting rules to reward longer holding periods help? Might quality voting sway indexers to focus more? Will robotic programmers and authors of AI deserve to earn more than CEOs? Would that be an occasion for joy or despair?

Appendix A: Research, Method, and Names

1. While AUM data were not explicitly given, we defined an equation to compute the quarterly capital invested by each 13F filer. Using the manager's identification number and stock holdings information, we aggregated quarterly holdings (shares owned multiplied by stock price) of each manager to compute quarterly AUM. To manage the data, at some cost in size skewing, only managers with average annual AUM (sum of quarterly AUM in a specific year divided by four quarters) exceeding $1 billion were retained.

2. Warren Buffett, "The Superinvestors of Graham and Doddsville," *Hermes*, May 17, 1984; Louis Lowenstein, "Searching for Rational Investors in a Perfect Storm," *Journal of Corporation Law* 30, no. 3 (2005): 539–59; Seth A. Klarman, "A Response to Lowenstein's Searching for Rational Investors in a Perfect Storm," *Journal of Corporation Law* 30, no. 3 (2005): 561–66; Bruce N. Greenwald, Judd Kahn, Paul D. Sonkin, and Michael van Biema, *Value Investing: From Graham to Buffett and Beyond* (Hoboken,

N.J.: Wiley, 2001), 159, 211–224; Allen C. Benello, Michael van Biema, and Tobias E. Carlisle, *Concentrated Investing: Investing Strategies of the World's Greatest Concentrated Investors* (Hoboken, N.J.: Wiley, 2016); John Train, *Money Masters of Our Time* (New York: HarperCollins, 2000), 306.

3. See Paul Borochin and Jie Yang, "The Effects of Institutional Investor Objectives on Firm Valuation and Governance," *Journal of Financial Economics* 126, no. 1 (2017): 171–99. The table highlighted the various QSs by portfolio size.

4. Martijn Cremers and Ankur Pareek, "Patient Capital Outperformance: The Investment Skill of High Active Share Managers Who Trade Infrequently," *Journal of Financial Economics* 122, no. 2 (2016): 288–306. The median concentration level is 79 percent, with the authors classifying those below 60 percent as closet indexers. The median holding period is 1.166 years (fourteen months), with the bottom quintile breakpoint being 0.483 (seven months). Holding periods have been fairly stable over time, though increasing in recent years.

Those with concentration scores above 0.96 are usually associated with special purposes, such as foundations whose portfolios are dominated by a single stock (Hershey Trust, Hewlett Foundation, Lilly Endowment); companies with large permanent stakes in publicly traded subsidiaries (Loews Corporation, Moody National Bank); and private equity firms with such transitional stakes (Apollo, Ares, Bain Capital, Thomas H. Lee Partners, General Atlantic, Pacific Financial).

5. See Jerker Denrell, "Vicarious Learning, Undersampling of Failure, and the Myths of Management," *Organization Science* 14, no. 3 (May–June 2003): 227–351; Jerker Denrell, "Should We Be Impressed with High Performance?," *Journal of Management Inquiry* 14, no. 3 (September 2005): 292–98.

Appendix B: Selected Quality Shareholder Statements

Adapted from Lawrence A. Cunningham, Torkell Eide, and Patrick Hargreaves, *Quality Investing: Owning the Best Companies for the Long Term* (London: Harriman, 2015). My co-authors on this book are investors with AKO Capital in London.

1. See Christian Caspar, Ana Karina Dias, and Heinz-Peter Elstrodt, "The Five Attributes of Enduring Family Businesses," McKinsey & Company, January 2010, https://www.mckinsey.com/business-functions/organization/our-insights/the-five-attributes-of-enduring-family-businesses.

Index

academic literature, indexing and, 22

accountability, 6, 25, 133, 163, 228n9

accounting, 86, 95–97, 142, 145. *See also* generally accepted accounting principles

Ackman, Bill, 16

acquisitions, 48–49, 70, 107–108, *108*, 111

active fund management, 188–189, 213n46

active proxy contests, 35

Active Share methodology, 194

activism, 35–38, 149, 203–204

activists, 3, 4, 17, 199; accountability and, 6, 163; director selection and, 130–131; hedge funds, 211n29; incumbents and, 25; influence of, 163; managers and, 20; ownership structure and, 35–36; QSs and, 6, 19–20, 164; rise of, 15; spin-offs and, 121; strategies of, 14–15, 36; transients and, *21*; voting and, 162

aggregate market, 28

AGM, 80–81

Airgas, 27

Air Liquide, 91, 224n13

Air Products, 27

AKO Capital, 187–188

Akre, Chuck, 44

Alibaba, 150

Alleghany Corporation, 62–63, 122

Alpha Architect (Gray), 22

Amazon.com, 26, 41, 68–69

American Tobacco, 140

America Online (AOL), 46

analysis, 168–169, 193, 200

Ang, Andrew, 213n46

annual growth rate, 13–14

Baruch, Bernard, 147
Baupost Group, 173
Belinfanti, Tamara, 208n8
benchmark skepticism, 196
Ben & Jerry's, 48, 78–79
Bergman, Stanley, 57–58
Berkshire Hathaway, 2–5, 34, 49,
  56–57, 75, 77, 173–174
Berman, Neuberger, 6, 36
Berra, Yogi, 66
Bethlehem Steel, 140
Bezos, Jeff, 26, 68–69
BlackRock, 29, 31, 61–62, 63,
  213n46
Bloomberg, Mike, 147
BNP Paribas, 91
boards: cap on serving on, 34;
  CEOs and, 132; CEO selection
  and, 129; compensation
  committees, 141; density and,
  227n8; director selection and,
  127; executive compensation
  and, 144; meeting agendas, 92;
  oversight, capital allocation
  and, 111–112; QSs on, 44;
  refreshment, 138; share
  buybacks and, 119; weakness,
  130. *See also* directors; director
  selection
Boeing, 127
Bogle, Jack, 15
bonuses, 140–141, 146
Boston Beer Company, 154
Boston Partners, 52
Boyar Value Group, 23
Bragg, Steven, 208n8
Brandeis, Louis, 141
branding, density and, *48*
brand managers, 219n20
British Petroleum, 81
Brooks, John, 76

Buffett, Warren, 2, 4, 34, 44,
  119, 173, 195, 207n3; annual
  letters of, 5, 68, 70; on capital
  allocation, 109; Coca-Cola and,
  58; on earnings smoothing,
  98; metrics of, 96; on share
  buybacks, 109
Building High Performance Boards,
  136
building value, 27
Burgundy, 52
Burns, John, 122
Bush, George W., 144
Bushee, Brian, 98, 208n8
Bush O'Donnell Investment
  Advisors, 189
business, 129, 191–192, 195, 198,
  200–201, 208n8
Business Roundtable, 57, 178, 180,
  220n3
buy and hold, 195, 197
buybacks, 29, 108–110, 119, 199,
  208n8, 226n6

Cable One, 29, 50
CAC-40, 156
capacity to reinvest, 64
capacity to suffer, 64, 198
capital allocation, 9, 29, 73, 99,
  132, 163, 164, 198; acquisitions
  and, 107–108, *108*; of AKO
  capital, 187; balance sheet
  and, 105; board oversight and,
  111–112; Buffett on, 109; cash
  flow and, 104; CEOs and, 100–
  101, 129, 225n1; consistency
  of, *106*; at Credit Acceptance
  Corporation, 112; definition of,
  101; dividends and, 110–111;
  effectiveness of, 102; excess
  cash, *102*; fluidity in, 105;

Warren Buffett Shareholder, The,
77–78
Wartzman, Rick, 221n4
Washington Post, 50
Washington Post Co., 29, 34, 49,
69, 70, 109, 144, 178
Watsa, Prema, 44, 59, 69, 80,
226n6
websites, of QSs, 186
Wellington, 216n17
Wells Fargo, 127

WeWork, 97
women, director selection and,
135–136
World War II, 13

XTRA, 224n2

Yale School of Management,
194

Zedge, 122